PEDAGOGY AND THE
POLITICS OF THE BODY

CRITICAL EDUCATION PRACTICE
VOLUME 16
GARLAND REFERENCE LIBRARY OF SOCIAL SCIENCE
VOLUME 1153

CRITICAL EDUCATION PRACTICE
SHIRLEY R. STEINBERG AND JOE L. KINCHELOE, SERIES EDITORS

Pedagogy and the Politics of the Body
A Critical praxis

Sherry B. Shapiro

Garland Publishing, Inc.
A member of the Taylor & Francis Group
New York and London
1999

Library of Congress Cataloging-in-Publication Data

Shapiro, Sherry B., 1952–
    Pedagogy and the politics of the body / by Sherry B. Shapiro.
        p.   cm. — (Garland reference library of social science ; v. 1153.
    Critical education practice ; v. 16)
        Includes index.
        ISBN 0-8153-2781-1 (alk. paper)
        1. Critical pedagogy.   2. Body, Human (Philosophy)   3. Feminism and
    education.   4. Dance—Study and teaching—Social aspects.   5. Education—
    Philosophy.   I. Title.   II. Series: Garland reference library of social
    science ; v. 1153.   III. Series: Garland reference library of social
    science.   Critical education practice ; vol. 16.
    LC196.S54   1999
    370.11'5—dc21   98–33338
                                                                                         CIP

Cover photo, *Censored,* by Lynn Leon.

Printed on acid-free, 250-year-life paper
Manufactured in the United States of America

*For Svi who helped me learn how to articulate
a language of embodied lived experience.*

Table of Contents

Foreword

Sherry Shapiro's book, *Pedagogy and the Politics of the Body*, is inspired by an acute and often painful realization that, no matter how distant, removed, and powerless human beings feel in relations to the complexity of contemporary social and economic life, they carry the mega- and microstructures of social life in the machinery of their flesh, in the pistons of their muscle, in the furnaces of their guts, and in the steely wires of their tendons. Shapiro both recognizes and affirms the primacy of the body in the creation of all knowledge. She further demands the inclusion of the human body as a nexus of textual production since she is aware that, produced within discourse, the body is also generative of discourse. Shapiro admonishes that educational theory doesn't place much importance on the body.

Merely to recognize the importance of the body in educational theorizing is to attract censure from the doyens of the educational establishment, but to affirm such a knowledge and render it valid—as does Shapiro—is firmly an act of apostasy. We all have unfinished business with the history or our body, and Shapiro provides us with an approach to map and transform such history.

The field of education needs impertinent and irreverent scholars like Sherry Shapiro. Her act of scholarship is both a reflective practice of resistance and a tactical engagement in transformation.

Shapiro's book is centered around resisting the injustice that our bodies know only too well through the sorrow and the suffering of the flesh. Our bodies, Shapiro opines, are being "skinned alive," inscribed by the productive processes that exploit human lives for economic purposes, violently inserting these bodies into the global division of labor. Shapiro is referring not only to individual bodies but collective bodies. The body, for Shapiro, is the prison house of injustice. We can see the history of injustice written into the steely eyes and sadistic grin of the Latinophobic, southland gringo politician; in the downcast eyes, heavy postures, and swollen faces of the people. Yet we also learn from Shapiro that the future is written into the body. We discern the glimmer of possible futures in the loving smile of a teacher in the thrall of a dialogical embrace of her students, in the improvised moves of a dancer in harmony with her surroundings, in the soothing words of friendship spoken from the heart to a person dying from AIDS, or in the shuddering currents of hate-filled pleasure (that have L.A.P.D. written all over them) that unleash a fury of baton swipes aimed at suspected "illegal" aliens.

Shapiro argues that all knowledge is body-mediated, that all learning is primarily somatic; that the act of knowing is largely a form of corporeal shaping in which women are transformed into objects of display and identity, their image circumscribed and policed by the male gaze. Corporeal shaping is particularly pronounced here in Los Angeles where getting buffed, toned, and ripped are prerequisites for attracting even a passing glance.

Shapiro is especially sensitive to how oppression is lived by the female body/subject, how women in particular have been transformed through a patriarchal will to dominate and to subjugate, into ornaments of male desire to be worn as decorative signs that signify male ownership and power. This will to dominate is facilitated by the Western counterpositioning of mind against body, fact against value, reason against the chaos of the emotions.

Drawing on the work of Andrea Dworkin, Frigga Haug, Maxine Greene, and others, Shapiro argues that "the objectification and oppression of women finds its parallel in the life of all human beings described as 'other'—for foreign-born workers, Jews, blacks, gays, those who are physical and mentally, differently abled—any human being who is dehumanized for the sake of another." Her message, grounded in materialist feminism and underwritten by a politics of liberation reminiscent of the work of Paulo Freire, is that educators and cultural workers who are compliant and collaborative with such dehumanization must hold themselves responsible for the "stripping away" of those possible futures arching towards hope. As a feminist, Shapiro sets out to "re-flesh" women who have been "skinned alive," that is, to create conditions of emancipation for those women whose bodily knowing and politics of location have been devalued, displaced, and de-legitimated through patriarchal relations of domination and oppression. More specifically, Shapiro is involved with women who struggle against the hegemony that inscribes the relationship between themselves and the world, a world that has grown increasingly sexist, racist, and class divided, a world less hospitable to social justice, to equality, to the struggle for freedom. Shapiro recognizes that hope must be dialectically reinitiated through a hieroglyphics of possibility pressed into the hearts and minds of the people, into the flesh of reason where dreams are released from the bondage of history and enter into the realm of the concrete.

Of course, criticalists in the field of education have struggled for decades against the steady erosion of civil rights and equality as these relationships are played out in the institutional and political life of schooling. But Shapiro recognizes that such a struggle, while admirable, is often itself predicated upon the very mind-body split that she is dedicated to overcoming, that as a "stepchild of modernist thinking," critical pedagogy recapitulates a pedagogical masculinity underwritten by devouring machineries of cynical reason. Many criticalists have participated in resurrecting, even as they claimed to oppose, the normalizing aspects of male privilege that they ostensibly wish to overcome.

Shapiro argues that our lives are dominated by a prevalent system of intelligibility that structures "seeing" as "knowing" and that this "seeing" sets itself in opposition to the female ways of knowing that are relational. Such seeing is linked, among other things, to occularcentrism as masculine forms of ownership. She writes that "the mode of exchange that organizes a standard human pleasure and desire is regulated by the masculine mode of desire." She speaks from a feminist epistemology that not only rejects the "prevalent masculine way of knowing" but develops a "relational" engagement with knowledge. In doing so, she vigorously attacks the disembodied discourse that scaffold official epistemological positions and legitimating objective knowledge.

Knowledge is as much about bone, gristle, and capillaries as it is about objective fact and universal value. Shapiro trenchantly adopts the position that "there is no view from nowhere," refusing the attractive allure of epistemological relativism that has enchanted so many educationalists who fancy themselves as liberal humanists. Shapiro knows better. She knows that the body/subject is always emplaced and placated in history, is always narrativized by discourse, is always already situated within cultural memory, within the seamless folds of the social. For instance, Shapiro understands how the social landscape of the classroom prepares students for their place within the social division of labor while naturalizing existing gender roles within patriarchy and within heteronormative discourses of power. She understands that the body-subject is an agonistic field of conflict, a contesting and contestatory site where flesh meets steel, where bone meets metaphor, where mind meets manure. Knowledge is never pristine and odor-free; it is always tainted and sometimes it stinks; it is enfleshed within systems and structures of domination, within criss-crossed vectors of power and asymmetrical relations of privilege. The map of knowledge is never clean, but always cross-hatched by lines of forces.

Not only does Shapiro navigate these lines and force fields of power that inscribe knowledge in the flesh, but she has lived within their vortex. Nobody ever escapes these fields unscathed and the outcome, while never irrevocably determined or predictable, is nevertheless overwhelmingly influenced under capitalism in the construction of ethnicity, class, gender, and sexual orientation. She sees the worlds of determinism (physical world) and indeterminism (subjective and social world) as mutually informing just as she sees meaning and matter as undeniably related to each other.

Shapiro advocates for the centrality of situated knowledge that is inscribed in the flesh, and for understanding how the body can become a vehicle for oppression but also for resistance and transformation. She further undertakes an exercise of "writing the body." In so doing, she attempts to redefine bodily knowledge outside of a mere technical discourse in order to lay the foundation of a critical discourse of the body.

Shapiro reinstates the body at the center of educational discourse. Because, for Shapiro, bodies are the primary means by which capitalism does its job, to develop a critical discourse of the body means mapping the body and the space in which it is fashioned. The body is produced in the image of capital but through the creation of a critical vernacular and praxis of liberation it can be reappropriated. Shapiro's own experiences as a dancer inform much of her theorizing, as she attempts to bring aesthetic feeling into the domain of ethical sensibility in order that educators and cultural workers can understand, name, and transform social life. The realm of the aesthetic is important because it links people through a type of sensuous belonging, yet it can also inscribe forms of social power—often malevolent— more deeply into our bodies, thereby increasing the social control of the state. Dancing, according to Shapiro, enables her "volatilized" body to locate itself in time and space in order to enact "a form of resistance to the separation of the mind and body, thought and feeling, creativity and existence." Of course, embodied actions such as those of dance are not ahistorical constants but are developed out of situated practices. Subjectivity itself has to be seen from this perspective as material, occurring in three-dimensional space and within the symbolic density of the process of signification.

We can trace philosophical attempts to break from the mind-body dualism to Spinoza, Nietzsche, and more recently, Deleuze. Spinoza, for instance, held that reason was the greatest power available to body/subjects, but that such reason is immanent, embodied, and enfleshed. For Spinoza, the mind is the idea of the body (Gatens, 1996). Spinoza posited an irreducible difference between bodies, and an absence of a common body. Since ethics or reason has its genesis in the body—and not, as Hegel claims, in the abstract individual—the absence of a collective body makes the Kantian notion of a universalized ethics produced by an autonomous will simply incoherent (Gatens, 1996). For Spinoza, necessity governs the mind and the passions of the body, and such necessity provides the conditions of possibility for free human activity. Analysis of the concrete must therefore proceed from an analysis of the passions and the imagination. Indeed, as Gatens illustrates, following Antonio Negri, politics must be seen as the metaphysics of the imagination, as the metaphysics of the human constitution of the world. If knowledge is embodied, then one would need to follow Spinoza in positing that all human relations are ethically structured.

Spinoza presumes a conception of the univocity of being. Following Spinoza, Moira Gatens (1996, p. 100) writes that "the ethics or reason which any particular collective body produces will bear the marks of that body's genesis, its (adequate or inadequate) understanding of itself, and will express the power or capacity of that body's endeavor to sustain its own integrity." It follows that criticalists must share an "embodied responsibility" for achieving and maintaining social justice within civil society.

In *Volatile Bodies*, Elizabeth Grosz, following Nietzsche, notes:

> Philosophy is a product of the body's impulses that have mistaken themselves for psyche or mind. Bodies construct systems of belief, knowledge, as a consequence of the impulses of their organs and processes. Among the belief systems that are the most pervasive, long-lived and useful are those grand metaphysical categories—truth, subject, morality, logic—which can all be read as bodily strategies, or rather resources which co-ordinate the will to power. (p. 124)

Elizabeth Grosz writes that for Nietzsche, beliefs "are adjuncts to the senses, modes of augmentation of their powers and capacities; and, like the senses, they yield interpretations, not truths, perspectives which may be life-enhancing which may favor movement, growth, vigor, expansion" (p. 127).

For Deleuze and Guattari, the body exists "as a surface of speeds and intensities before it is stratified, unified, organized, and hierarchized" (Grosz, 1994, p. 169). Grosz argues that bodies are constituted by alterity, which is both the condition for and result of embodiment. She is worth quoting at length:

> Bodies themselves, in their materialities, are never self-present... because embodiment, corporeality, insist on alterity.... Alterity is the very possibility and process of embodiment: it conditions but is also a product of the pliability or plasticity of bodies which makes them other than themselves, other than their "nature," their functions and identities. (p. 209)

In his book, *The Body in Late-Capitalist U.S.A.*, Donald M. Lowe examines the intersection among body practices, work habits, language, and the social relations of production and consumption and argues that capital and the body constitutes a new binary opposition in which the body acts as the "other" to late-capitalist development. Late-capitalist accumulation depends upon the exploitation of bodily needs and of non-exchangist values. Lowe further notes that "the unequal development of valorized lifestyles, social reproduction, gender, sexuality, and psychopathology displaces and camouflages the unequal social relations of production" (1995, p. 174). In order to resist the means/ends relations in the late-capitalist opposition between bodily needs and capital accumulation we need to recode the issues of bodily needs provoked by the hegemony of exchangist practices (Lowe, 1995, pp. 175-176).

An important direction taken by Shapiro is her attempt to develop a critical pedagogy of the body. According to Shapiro, social relations of exploitation and enforced poverty are naturalized as they partake of an unspoken allure of commonsense knowledge and received meaning. Shapiro's pedagogy of corporeal resistance—what she calls a "choreographic/pedagogic project" consists of strategies of rupture, decentering, and textuality that focus on the intersection of bodily knowledge and the repressed social order. Yet Shapiro is not content with a pedagogy

that offers only oppositional readings of social and cultural antag-
onisms; rather, she is interested in developing concrete strategies
and tactics of resistance and transformation at the level of representations, institutional practices, and social and cultural relations. Shapiro's critical pedagogy is a site-specific cultural politics that concerns itself with decentering dominant systems of
classifications as well as the current global political economy; in
other words, it is a pedagogy that is designed to contest social
relations informed by a white-supremacist patriarchal capitalism.
It is a pedagogy that attempts to break through the motivated
amnesia of body-subjects unable to even look upon the images of
homeless crowding the parks and streets, in order to rouse bodies
into acts of resistance and liberation. Such a pedagogy of liberation must involve economic restructuring as well as discursive
and symbolic path-making. Shapiro recognizes that patterns of
distribution, division of labor, and relations of production and
consumption figure prominently in such a pedagogy.

In Judith Butler's (1993) terms, Shapiro is calling forward a
pedagogy of radical resignification, a restorative dismantling and
reassemblage of subjectivity, a substantial remaking of the subject. As part of a critical pedagogy, counterhegemonic practices
must take into account and contest specific practices of bodies,
such as those created by phallo-militaristic machineries of fascist
desire that—as recent history attests—are more than incipient
possibilities here in Los Angeles and elsewhere throughout the
United States.

Sherry Shapiro's pedagogy does not follow a Platonic logic;
in other words, it is not merely about a "lack" between present
circumstances and an imaginary representation of that which we
do not possess in concrete reality. Rather, she recognizes that the
so-called lack is itself an historical and social production and not
some universal prerequisite for fulfillment. Consumer "lacks" are
always already installed within contemporary forms of global
capitalism. Everything within capitalism conspires to conceal
how the body is ordered symbolically in accordance with the
desiring-production of the marketplace. Such a pedagogy, in
assuming responsibility for the embodied history of the civil

body, strives for new relations of sociability that work to confront and contest the political-economic arrangements designed to serve and protect mainly white males. Readers are provoked to ask: How might human relations be restructured and re-embodied outside of appeals to transcendent moral or religious categories and from the perspective of a community of rational and sensual beings? (Gatens, 1996)

Sherry Shapiro has written an engaging book that resituates the struggle for freedom in both the hope and the promise of the senses and the ethical sway of the political imagination. It is a book that invites educators and cultural workers to develop new forms of self-fashioning, new modalities of sense-making, and new social formation of collective struggle.

Peter McLaren
Los Angeles, 1997

Preface

This book represents the work of eight years of focusing on the body as this intersects with questions of pedagogy, art, and social change. The intellectual endeavor grew out of many more years experiencing my body as a dancer. If there was a watershed moment in this process in which the rational and sensual seemed to come together, it was in the office of one of my doctoral professors when he asked, "How do you think about your body?" My quick reply was, "We don't think about our bodies in dance!" Dissatisfied with my own response, I began to question why we didn't think about our bodies—other than as objects for technical proficiency. I had become conscious of my own alienation.

I began, in my doctoral work, making connections between the individual and the social, the rational and the sensual, art and life. Wanting to value both my intellectual self, an aspect which had been denied as a female, and my embodied self, an aspect denied as a dancer, I tried to do what I named at the time as "reclamation." I wanted to reclaim my intellectuality and keep the awareness that is mediated through the body. From that point forward, I have been creating a pedagogic process that gives attention to the project of liberation in a way that takes seriously the body as a site for self and social transformation. This book reflects my struggles to do just that—to create a process where the "body/subject" becomes a means for producing liberatory knowledge about the person and the culture. *As such, it examines what it might mean to approach questions of identity, justice, moral responsibility, ideological conformity, and resistance through an engagement with our own body experiences and memories.* In particular this book tries to lay the foundation for a theory and practice of a somatically-oriented critical pedagogy. While recent writers in education (especially those concerned with the postmodern) have emphasized the significance of the body as a focus of cultural inscription and power, there have been only a few real attempts to follow through on such a perspective and elaborate what it would mean to teach critically about, and through, the body.

The chapters range across a number of discourses; education, art and the aesthetic, dance, the history of philosophy, and popular culture. They emphasize the way the body—especially the female body—is shaped and reshaped to the ideological contours of the existing society. Noting how the body is not only inscribed by power, but also expresses resistance to a hegemonic culture, I attempt to create a dialogue between embodied knowing and cultural critique. I suggest that the body is always a locus of freedom, pleasure, connection and creativity, and that a critical pedagogy of the body means to understand not only how it is socialized into heteronomous relations of control and conformity, but is also a site of struggle and possibility for a more liberated and erotic way of being in the world. In all of this, the book lays out the argument for an expanded, sensuous notion of knowing and learning, and the way this might relate to existing traditions of critical and emancipatory education.

The diversity of writing styles reflects the nature of this project; moving from the analytic to the phenomenological, to evocative description forms. The latter help us to convey in personal language what it means to critically reflect on our lives as enfleshed creatures, and also to capture the mood and sense of my choreographic work. In chapter one, "Thinking About Thinking," I draw upon the work of Martin Heidegger to begin an examination of the Western philosophical tradition as a foundation for questioning those aspects of critical pedagogy which continue to be shaped by dualistic notions of mind and body. Utilizing the work of Paulo Freire, Maxine Greene, Peter McLaren, Kathleen Weiler and others who have been engaged in connecting education theory to the larger concern for human liberation, I provide a perspective which calls into question any approach committed to human liberation which does not seriously address the "body" as a site for both liberation and oppression. I contend that human liberation significantly depends on the struggle to achieve critical awareness of our "embodied knowledge." Developing out of both Foucauldian and feminist traditions, the body/subject, is viewed as both socially inscribed and managed. It is this understanding which provides the basis for a critical pedagogy which addresses itself to, and is reflective upon, the body in contemporary culture.

Chapter two, "The Body and Knowledge: Towards Relational Understanding," explores the epistemological subordination of a concrete language of the body, or sensate lived-experience. The order of the "rational" over the "irrational" is brought into question as I review the historical and philosophical underpinnings of thinking. Questions concerning the dominant paradigm of knowing is addressed in the context of the sociology of the body, feminist and critical theories, as well as Heidegger's work on thinking.

"Skinned Alive: Towards A Postmodern Pedagogy of the Body," chapter three, explores the work of a number of commentators who have developed a discourse of the body and struggled to provide a framework for understanding embodied knowledge. Following previous arguments concerning the importance of an embodied, critical discourse, this chapter provides a sense of how we might begin to broaden our understandings of lived experience through a language made sensuous and corporeal. I have looked here to the work of Andrea Dworkin, Don Johnson, Toni Morrison, John Berger, Helene Cixous and others. The intention is to employ such a language in discovering deeper possibilities for contesting the experience and structures of oppression and authority as these are manifested in patriarchal, classist and homophobic society.

Chapter four, "Re-Membering the Body in Critical Pedagogy," continues to look at the inadequacy of much of the current theoretical discourse of critical pedagogy. Utilizing current feminist and postmodern critiques, I focus upon the body's role in the process of knowing and in the praxis of freedom.

Much of the chapter consists of a series of my own reflections on the way in which subjectivity and identity are formed through the body's situatedness within the culture. I combine personal narrative with social critique illustrating how such reflections can produce a language of cultural understanding. Particularly, this critical process of coming to know brings together the traditions of both feminist and critical theory through the use of personal narrative, embodied knowledge, and cultural understandings. These traditions have sought to bring to consciousness the way in which personal experience mediates social relationships, especially those concerned with power or domination.

In chapter five, "An Existential Look: Research As Praxis," I discuss a research study concerned with the life histories of three dancers. The study attempts to provide an example of research as praxis—that is research which has, as its purpose, dialogue, that engages participants in questions that make possible self and social change. Going beyond the purely phenomenological approach, it attempts to relate experience to cultural context clarifying the ways in which dance mediates both practices of social conformity *and* liberation. Questions in this study relate to existential issues, such as identity, home, individualism, the female body (tracing the traditions of women in dance as patterned by the larger culture), and the understanding of aesthetics as a potential practice of freedom.

Following from this, chapter six, "Reaching Beyond the Familiar; Redefining Dance Education as an Emancipatory Pedagogy," critiques the dominant discourse of dance and attempts to redefine dance education as an emancipatory pedagogy. Central to this is a conceptual schema (drawing upon Habermas' contrasting bases for the production of knowledge) that lays out the alternative discourses which structure pedagogies of dance. These include the technical-authoritarian; the creative (understood in the 19th century aesthetic romantic mode); and an emergent participatory-emancipatory form of learning.

In the final chapter, I return to a specific focus on a critical pedagogy of the body. I attempt to look at the theoretical and practical implications of such a pedagogy and address questions raised within feminist and postmodern discourses. These questions examine the use of power by critical pedagogues themselves, and the potential hazards of their own use of authority. There is also the danger in postmodern theories of the loss of any meaningful subjectivity, and thus the exclusion of any real notion of a body/subject from which human actions and creativity emanate. As an advocate of critical pedagogy, I seek to draw upon re-membering as an act of re-identifying the self in all of its creative, critical, and ethical dimensions; a process in which the self might find a home in this torn and afflicted world. The task is larger than a cognitive repositioning of the historical and cultural subject. No longer can we suggest that the ability to rationally apprehend is enough. A pedagogy concerned with human liberation must insist upon a sensual language and practice for education, which may evoke among our students a passion for love, justice, and the sense of what it might mean to live purposeful lives.

I would like to express my solidarity with those who continue to struggle for an education which is critical, creative and moral; and express my gratitude for their ideas, conversations, encouragement, and support. I would like to thank my students who have traveled with me on my journeys, given me great trust, and acted with courage. I would also like to thank Svi, without his questions, editing, and love this book would not have happened.

About the Cover Artist

Lynn Leon was born in Tynemouth, England. She studied Fine Art (photography) at the University of Northumbria at Newcastle where she attained her Master of Arts degree. She lives and works in North Yorkshire but travels frequently to Israel where she photographs, draws, and exhibits her artwork.

Her work from the mid-1980's consists of large composite black and white photographs which explore the nature of confinement and violence, whilst also dealing with the vulnerability of the female body. Some of her images contain references both to the Holocaust and to the latent tensions in Israel.

Her more recent work—small pen and ink drawings—are directly concerned with the political situation in Israel and are therefore more topical and provocative. She uses her Jewishness, her belief in the Middle-East peace process, and her interest in Surrealism as a basis for her work.

Lynn Leon has exhibited widely in England and Israel. Her photographs and drawings were represented in the "Rubies and Rebels" exhibition at the Barbican in London in 1996. Her image "Censored" was used in all the publicity for this major exhibition. It was the first exhibition of its kind to deal with "Jewish Female Identity in Contemporary British Art."

Lynn Leon has work in a number of collections in the United States, the United Kingdom, and Israel.

Historians long ago began to write of the body. They have studied the body in the field of historical demography or pathology; they have considered it as the seat of needs and appetites, as the locus of physiological processes and metabolisms, a target for the attacks of germs or viruses; they have shown to what extent historical processes were involved in what might seem to be the purely biological base of existence; and what place should be given in the history of society to biological "events" such as the circulation of bacilli, or the extension of the lifespan. But the body is also directly involved in a political field; power relations have an immediate hold upon it; they invest it, mark it, train it, torture it, force it to carry out tasks to perform ceremonies, to emit signs.

—Michel Foucault, *Discipline and Punish*

As a stubbornly local phenomenon, the body fits well enough with postmodern suspicions of grand narratives, as well as with pragmatism's love affair with the concrete. Since I know where my left foot is at any particular moment without needing to use a compass, the body offers a mode of cognition more intimate and internal than a now much-scorned Enlightenment rationality.

—Terry Eagleton, *The Illusions of Postmodernism*

I think, therefore I am is the statement of an intellectual who underrates toothaches. *I feel, therefore I am* is a truth much more universally valid, and it applies to everything that's alive.

—Milan Kundera, *Immortality*

PEDAGOGY AND THE POLITICS OF THE BODY

CHAPTER ONE

Thinking about Thinking

[T]he most thought-provoking thing about our thought-provoking age is that we are still not thinking.... Thinking is not so much an act as a way of living...a way of life. It is a remembering who we are as human beings and where we belong. It is a gathering and focusing of our whole selves on what lies before us; a taking to heart and mind these particular things before us in order to discover them in their essential nature and truth. (Martin Heidegger, *What is Called Thinking*)

Martin Heidegger (1968) brings our attention to the dialectical relationship between "how we think" and "how we live." He reminds us that our being-in-the-world is one of relationship to others and to the larger world. What is to be uncovered in relationship are the "truths" of human existence; that which lies before us. There is no final or absolute "Truth," but there are "truths." At the same time there is an undeniable reality to existence. This is the social and institutional reality that confronts human beings in their everyday lives—a reality that cannot be ignored or forgotten without punishment. Cornel West (1988) speaks to the "realness" that is found in our everyday lives:

There is a reality that one cannot not know. The ragged edges of the Real, of Necessity, not being able to eat, not having shelter, not having health care, all this is something that one cannot not know. (p. 277)

West (1988) speaks out of that neo-pragmatist tradition that calls into question any claims to truth or reality separated from the social practices from which they are produced. Rejected is the notion of a transcendent reality or ahistorical truth, which have so dominated our philosophical traditions in the West and hidden the connections between knowledge sought and knowledge gained, and the knower and the known (Sandra Bartky, 1990). Under the influence of postmodern thinking recent educational and philosophical conversations have been engaged in a paradigm shift questioning any "totalizing" theory. Not only have particular theoretical perspectives been challenged but so have knowledge claims that aren't culturally and historically situated. Challenged by Heidegger's work, one can no longer think in terms of purified abstractions; rather truth, being, and existence are to be understood as a single event. And further, events, truths, or reality can be better understood through a critical understanding of the individual/social relationship. Understanding of such social relationships requires a critical way of thinking that recognizes and brings to awareness human participation in the co-creation of life as it presently exists.

Most poetically, Heidegger's "ways of thinking" call us back to think with our heart, to hear the most primal call, the call of Being. He brings together the critical, creative, and moral aspects of thinking and unifies them into a philosophy that is ontologically, rather than epistemologically, oriented. The power underlying Heidegger's question, "What is called thinking?" is in his desire to recall the original question of being. This question unites us as humans with a responsibility for ourselves and the world in which we live. This ontological understanding is one in which, Heidegger asserts, thinking and questioning are inherent in being-in-the-world. Questioning leads the way of thinking about our lives and the world in which we live. In connecting what we care about to what and how we question, Heidegger reasserts the importance of the relationship between the structuring of the question (what we both know and desire to know) to the answers or realities we find. This shift from epistemology to ontology suggests that the manner in which we construct and validate knowledge or knowing is related to how we construct reality or experience. Thinking and being are, in a sense, one in the same.

In Old English, as reflected in Heidegger's work (p. 139) thinking is referenced to the word "Thanc," which means memory; as a thinking that recalls the gift of thinking and gives thanks for it. Heidegger (1968) writes:

> The thanc, the heart's core, is the gathering of all that concerns us, all that we care for, all that touches us insofar as we are, as human beings. What touches us in the sense that it defines and determines our nature, what we care for, we might call contiguous or contact.... Only because we are by nature gathered in contiguity can we remain concentrated on what is at once present and past to come. The word "memory" originally means this incessant concentration on contiguity. In its original telling sense, memory means as much as devotion.... The *thanc* unfolds in memory, which persists as devotion. (pp. 144-145)

Human consciousness *is* constituted through memory. "Devotion" here can be thought of as the human desire to "make sense" of life, in ways that it connects to feelings of care and concern. This contiguity Heidegger speaks of is the relationship between all that we touch and all that touches us. Touching can be imaged as all that concerns us in the "everydayness" of our lives. The relationship is one between all that is the subject/object—human/other/world relationship. In this sense, the thinking of wo/man recalls her or his own ability to hold close those things we come to care for and be concerned about. These things are to be known as all inclusive of ourselves and our relationship to others and the larger world. Further, we are to remember that our humanness depends on our construction of these relationships into "a way of living." In so doing, one devotes oneself to the memory of what has been taken to heart; all that touches us insofar as we are human beings. In giving thanks, the heart recalls where it remains gathered and concentrated. It belongs in acknowledgment of relationship. For Heidegger, the human condition is based on our ability, not to reject history, but to understand that human beings carry within them their history into the present. From this present, we create our future through projections from this historical context (Seidel, 1964). Here there is a place that is "real" enough—one that speaks to the continual dialectic between individual experience and the conditions and circumstances of our lives.

Why start with Heidegger's work? This can only be explained in the context of my own life experiences through which my readings were interpreted at the time of this writing. Growing up during the 1950s and 1960s in the Western Appalachian mountains of North Carolina, I came to understand my body as something strong, even powerful. The experiences of exploring trails through woods, swinging from grapevines, making houses from fallen leaves, and lying on damp moss, all taught me to understand my world through sensual experience. Coming to know was certainly an *embodied* experience. Truth, limits, and possibilities were composed through experience. Freedom was something felt—exhilarating, breathtaking, and powerful. Early in my forming, I learned that freedom came out of decided action and risk taking. I also learned that it felt liberating. In reading Heidegger, I found affirmation of a way of knowing that wasn't objective, something only outside myself, but something that included me, my own experiences. I learned not only about the woods, trees, and earth; I learned about myself as I felt these things. My being-in-the-world was meaningful, my presence necessary to bring the world into being (not meant in the anthropomorphic sense). What I mean by this is that my sensual understandings had immense importance in the structuring of my being, and just how it is that I relate to others and the environment. My body was the mediator of experience, and knowledge was subjective. Entering school, I learned that coming to know was not inclusive of body knowledge. My physical being, which felt pain, joy, tiredness, exasperation, love, and energy, possibility and freedom, was to be ignored, even controlled. Indeed, I came to understand my body as some "thing" to be controlled. And sensual knowing was simply excised from the process of learning. Philosophically speaking, my body became *it*, rather than *is*; knowledge as objective, rather than subjective.

I turned to dance classes that involved body knowledge, even if in a technical way. Unfortunately, dance did not escape the reach of the instrumental rationality that was pervasive, and continues to be, in the field of education and arts. My body was an object for the gaining of technical skills. "It" was to learn to do the steps, mirroring the teacher, replicating the knowledge given. Yet the reunion of body and action in dance, contrary to schooling, did give me immense pleasure. I felt the connections between them. It was a confirmation of knowing and doing. Somewhere in these experiences, I was able to sense the relationship between power and possibility. Clearly, I understood the relationship between present action and future possibility as something that was influenced by me. Later in my life, as a woman and dancer, I experienced dance as oppositional, in some ways, to the dominant ideology for women, because dancing is about taking up space, defying stasis, being strong, and bending of the "normal" images and relationships of what "gendered" human beings can be and do. (Note here that both male and female images in dance are also highly problematic. I return to discuss this issue in later chapters.) Dance was a place where I could remember my body, and experience myself as whole again.

Growing up female during this time in history also meant a particular understanding of what the future concerns of a woman needed to be. My mother introduced me at the age of 18 to a 35-year-old man, saying, "Sherry, he is a millionaire." (We both "understood" what this meant. What more could a girl want? A rich man was certainly the "best" you could do.) My parent's response to higher education for me was, "If you want to go to college you will have to find a way to pay for it." It wasn't simply that I was female. It was that I was "artistic" and "pretty." Inherent in the messages, blatantly stated, was, "Why go to school, when you have the looks to get a rich husband?" and "Dancers are not academically smart." Intellectual scholarship or theory was something with which I was not to be concerned. Denied body in schooling (in the public sphere) and mind in the social construction of women's identity (in the private sphere), I struggled to overcome the painful denial of what I felt myself to be.

Somewhere embedded in my corporeal memories, I drew on body knowledge that "reminded" me of risk taking and possibility. Eventually (after the birth of two sons; two marriages, neither to rich men; and two divorces; a book in itself) I did complete my degrees and entered a doctoral program where, for the first time in education, I was introduced to critical thinking and discourses concerned with human meaning and existence. Starved of theoretical knowledge, I devoured them. Drawn to questions of meaningful existence, I found existential discourse as a powerful source to examine my own life. In Heidegger's work, the concept of "being-in-the-world," with its strong opposition to institutional conditions that required an unthoughtful acceptance of one's life and reality, provided a philosophically resonant place for me to begin to contemplate the human condition. What I later learned from Marx and feminist theory was to make that place more concrete. I also resonated with Heidegger's understanding of truth to be found in the relationship *between* subjects and objects; truth is about *who we are* as human beings not *what we are*. It is a way of finding truth that depends upon an understanding of ourselves as we relate to others. His explanation of "being-in-time" places humans always within a historical narrative where one carries one history into the present and projects into the future. Here is where conscious possibility is found, in "remembering" the past and imaging the future. In this work a space was opened for me to begin to resolve the mind/body split; where subjective knowledge could begin to be valued, "Truth" questioned, and human agency embraced and positioned within the context of future possibility.

Education and Critical Theory: Finding the Structures
For one year I took Heidegger's work to bed with me. I read and reread. Yet while studying I became dissatisfied with the referencing self, the authentic being (a term commonly called "authentic movement" in dance). This Self, as noted in Hannah Arendt's work (Young-Bruehl, 1982, p. 76), has as its most essential characteristic, "its absolute egoism, its radical separation from all its fellows." Even where Heidegger posits the value of human sociality, it is historically undifferentiated and institutionally unsubstantiated (maybe this is how he could embrace the Nazi *volk* so easily). It is precisely in this silence that my encounters with Marxism, critical theory, and feminism were

made so powerful. For here in their different ways were clearly indicated structures of human experience and oppression—historically and sociologically specific. Marxism taught me to understand the immense power of capitalism in shaping human life; and feminism, the pervasiveness of patriarchal domination. Each insisted that the point of sociopolitical analysis was not merely to understand the world but to change it. They provided discourses of critique and of possibility. Feminism, in particular, also radically expanded my language of social transformation, making it possible for me to integrate consciously into my work, and my life, notions of compassion, love, and justice.

As an educator and dancer, I began to seriously rethink how, in Western philosophical tradition, sensual knowledge was abstracted from what is called "thinking." As a woman and dancer my only recourse was to reclaim that which had been taken away. No longer would I be left out of the epistemological conversation; I was determined to reclaim thinking in terms that would acknowledge and affirm what I understood so powerfully, body knowledge. As I gained insight into my own ignorance of and compliance with the oppressing structure, I began to search for another story. I was not seeking a "born-again experience." What I needed was the ability to make choices that were liberatory and somewhat consistent with my strong sensibilities. It was in critical theory that I was able to ground my philosophy, meet radical democracy, and begin to understand the dynamics of human oppression and alienation in ways more grounded than I had previously seen them (Kanpol & McLaren, 1995). The direction of my existential concerns and pedagogic concerns converged. In encountering other critical educators, I discovered the possibility of integrating my concerns about human existence with questions of pedagogy. At the risk of covering ground that is familiar to some of the readers, I want to return to some of the key ides and insights of these writers.

Critical pedagogy theoretically developed and drew from a number of perspectives including the social reconstructionism of Dewey, the Frankfurt School of critical theory, democratic theory, feminist and cultural studies, and more recently, postmodern ideas and perspectives (McLaren, 1994). Characteristic of these disciplines or perspectives is the concern for the problematization of the concrete relations between the individual and the cultural forms in which they exist. Critical pedagogy starts from a critique of schooling in terms of its role in the shaping of subjectivity for a particular form of social life. Implied in this view is the recognition of the way existing social structures reproduce and perpetuate racism, sexism, and the inequalities of the class structure. Kathleen Weiler (1988) notes, "what essentially defines critical educational theory is its moral imperative and its emphasis on the need for both individual empowerment and social transformation (p. 6)." Critical pedagogy as a philosophy of praxis actively induces a dialogue that struggles with competing concepts of "how to live meaningfully in a world confronted by pain, suffering, and injustice" (Hammer & McLaren, 1989, p. 39). Pedagogy here is not to be equated narrowly with instructional practices. It includes the total reality of the classroom and a critique of how that reality comes to be formed through the integrating of a particular curriculum content and design, classroom strategies and techniques, and methods of evaluation, purpose, and selection of texts. Together they produce a particular ideological version of what knowledge has the most worth; who has the knowledge; what it means to know something; and how we use that knowledge to construct or reconstruct ourselves, others, and our environment. Students' experiences must be analyzed to understand how those experiences were shaped, produced, legitimated, or disconfirmed in reference to the dominant forms of knowledge. As Roger Simon (1987) writes:

> In other words, talk about pedagogy is simultaneously talk about the details of what students and others might do together and the cultural politics such practices support. In this perspective, we cannot talk about teaching practices without talking about politics. (p. 370)

Critical pedagogy takes to heart the possibility of education engaging in a process of human liberation for social transformation. It speaks with a vision of, and commitment to education, with this as its central purpose. Peter McLaren (1989) gives words to the foundational principles.

> Critical pedagogy resonates with the sensibility of the Hebrew symbol of "tikkun", which means "to heal, repair, and transform the world. All the rest is commentary." It provides historical, cultural, political, and ethical direction for those in education who still dare to hope. Irrevocably committed to the side of the oppressed, critical pedagogy is as revolutionary as the earlier views of the authors of the Declaration of Independence: since history is fundamentally open to change, liberation is an authentic goal, and a radically different world can be brought into being. (p. 160)

The connection between critical pedagogy and the Heideggerian sensibility for thinking is in the understanding that "how we think" is implicated in "how we live." This critical remembering of existence is the crucial departure and returning point for all inquiries into how we create our own lives and the lives of others. Critical inquiry becomes an integral part of revealing the interaction between the student's individual life and the society in which it is formed. Critical pedagogy concerns itself with "problematizing" the students' lives in the context of their world. Essential to this is a critical understanding through which students come to "make sense" of their lives through an awareness of the dialectical relationship between their subjectivity and the dominant culture. Central to this is the validation of personal knowledge and the concept of empowerment through which individuals "find their voices," (a common phrase used by critical pedagogues, which refers to creating spaces in the classroom for students to articulate their thoughts, concerns, ideas, feelings, and yearnings). Their voices articulate both a critical language and a language of possibility.

The purposeful question from which so many other questions originate is the question of being, living as such, making concrete one's own existence. In recognizing the essential question of being, critical pedagogy follows Heidegger's concern, but extends it into a deeper analysis of social institutions and an emancipatory vision of self and social transformation. It is dedi-

cated to critical understanding and the project of human liberation. It gives attention to "the way," or the journey that takes us
out of alienation and to some significant apprehension of the
meaning of our lives (Bruss & Macedol, 1985).

Perspectives on Critical Pedagogy

To understand how pedagogical practices represents a particular
politics of experience, Henry Giroux (1985) argues that

> critical educators need to develop a discourse that can be used to
> interrogate schools as ideological and material embodiments of a
> complex web of relations of culture and power, on the one hand, and
> as socially constructed sites of contestation actively involved in the
> production of lived experiences on the other. (p. 23)

Underlying Giroux's argument is one that points to "problematizing" and interrogating everyday classroom experiences; how
they are produced, interpreted, accepted, contested, and/or legitimated. Most simply, it is a recognition that schools embody the
politics of the culture from which they are formed. Svi Shapiro
(1989) defines culture as

> the terrain of struggle and contestation in which the subordinate and
> the oppressed constantly produce counter values, beliefs, images and
> ways of thinking that question and challenge domination, injustice,
> and alienation. (p. 81)

The discourse needed directs us towards the concept of cultural
literacy where the meanings embedded in the dominant and subordinate cultures are exposed and discussed in their knowl-
edge/power relationships. Cultural literacy is a reading of personal experiences as they are formed by the dominant culture.
"Dominant" refers to social practices, social forms, and social
structures that affirm the central values, interests, and concerns of
the social interest in control of the material and symbolic wealth
in society (Nieto, 1996). Giroux and Simon (1988) note that a
starting point for the critical pedagogical encounter is in popular
culture—the "terrain of images, knowledge forms, and affective

investments which define the ground on which one's 'voice' becomes possible" (p. 16). Individual voices must be understood within their cultural grounding. Critical pedagogy refers to this process as giving voice to one's own experiences by articulating the "reality" of one's life; coming to critical understanding of the sociocultural mapping of consciousness; and using individual voices collectively to struggle in the retelling and remaking of life stories. More recently the postmodern turn in critical pedagogy has emphasized the importance of challenging those "normalizing" voices of authority and knowledge. It has made clear that culture comprises a multiplicity of voices and identities, many of which are suppressed or invalidated. More than this it has shown us how much these identities come into being and continue through relationships with others. That is to say, there is no such thing as a sealed or essential cultural identity, only the constant play and interaction of diverse people marking out spaces of value and power. What Giroux and others call "border pedagogy" is the attempt to understand and become sensitive to the connections and separations that mark the conflict-filled terrain of our social lives. Giroux expresses it this way:

> Border literacy calls for pedagogical conditions in which differences are recognized, exchanged and mixed in identities that break down but are not lost, that connect but remain diverse... Underlying this notion of border pedagogy and literacy is neither the logic of assimilation (the melting pot), nor the imperative to create cultural hierarchies, but the attempt to expand the possibilities for different groups to enter into dialogue in order to further understand the richness of their differences and the value of what they share in common. (in Kanpol & McLaren, 1995, p. 121)

Reading critical theorists' work and understanding their rejection of the tenets of the traditional patriarchal educational system, as well as their concern for bringing to the core of the curriculum the lives of the students themselves, I began to understand that what was being offered was the substantiation of experience and the beginnings of an analysis of the social construction of those experiences (Middleton, 1993). The stories, told by students, are to be examined for their underlying assumptions, what was voiced and what was silenced, and what they divulge about our cultural experiences.

Such a process can be understood when returning to Paulo Freire's work, where literacy became connected to questioning and understanding lives in the context of a people's politics and culture. Freire (1988) called for a pedagogy that leaves behind what he calls the "banking" concept of schooling, in which students become depositories for a set knowledge imposed by teachers. He asserted the need to replace this concept of schooling with one in which

- the purpose of education is to empower students for personal and social transformation;
- the curriculum is always connected to the concrete issues of the student's life;
- critical thinking is a way of finding one's own voice within the individual/social dialogue;
- critical understanding is a foundational process in meaning-making in one's own life; and
- critical and creative consciousness are reunited in imaging a moral vision for a more fully human life.

Freire's notion of transformation brings to the conversation a hermeneutic process of attending to, reflecting upon, and interpreting reality as we know it. Beyond interpretation is the moral intention for change from "what is" to "what ought to be." David Purpel (1989) echoes this transformative theme: "curriculum for justice and social passion unites serious social criticism with possibilities for an alternative community based on ethical principles" (p. 162). Giroux and Simon (1988) summarize the concerns of education that is organized around critical pedagogy.

> This means that teaching and learning must be linked to the goals of educating students: to understand why things are the way they are and how they got to be that way; to make the familiar strange and the strange familiar; to take risks and struggle with ongoing relations of

power from within a life-affirming moral culture; and to envisage a world which is "not yet" in order to enhance the conditions for improving the grounds upon which life is lived. (p. 13)

Such a pedagogy engaged in ideological critique inevitably raises moral concerns. It exposes questions of social injustice, inequality, asymmetrical power, and the lack of human rights or dignity. This kind of education is at once both a political and a moral challenge. Svi Shapiro (1989) distinguishes the curricular concerns of a critical cultural literacy with its "social-interventionist" intent.

At the core of the social-interventionist approach to curricular knowledge is the notion of cultural literacy. Its central concern is not the accumulation of discrete skills or the segmented topics of sub-oriented schooling, but broad apprehension of the social/cultural formation which structures our everyday world. In this sense the curriculum is concerned with the connection of human practices among and between the moral/cultural, the political, the economic, the religious, the artistic and literary, and elsewhere. It must also emphasize, in the study of these spheres, the need for critical insight—awareness that penetrates the ideology of surface description in which our world is named in partial and distorting ways. Of course, a cultural literacy that attempts to provide critical awareness of the social/cultural formation cannot be a continuation of the remote abstractions of liberal arts tradition. It must, instead, be deeply rooted in the experience of individuals daily struggling with the crises of survival—material, moral, spiritual, and psychological. (p. 11)

Education, in the critical sense, focuses on the relationship between the individual's experiences and the sociohistorical context within which the experience is produced. It speaks a language developed out of everyday experience; the experience of "what is." Yet this is only one side of the coin. Shapiro (1989) explains, "Social-interventionist pedagogy is concerned with both what is and what might be. While the first face is analytic and relentlessly probing, the latter face is creative, imaginative, and also, hopeful" (p. 10).

For students to be able to engage in critical reflection requires a certain belief or faith. Kathleen Weiler (1988) writes that the single most important assumption of Giroux's educational theory is the "belief in each person's ability to understand and critique his or her own experiences and the social reality 'out there' that any project of pedagogical and ultimately social transformation rests on" (p. 23). What is significant to critical pedagogy is the belief in the capacity of individuals to act and react upon the social world they inhabit. Hegemony or domination is never complete but always in a process of being reimposed, *yet always capable of being resisted by historical subjects* (Brosio, 1994).

Antonio Gramsci's analysis of social consciousness as an organizing but resisted principle of everyday life has allowed radical educators to develop the concept of counter-hegemony. Purpel and Shapiro (1995) calls for the work of critical teachers to be viewed as counter-hegemonic, recognizing not only the structural constraints under which they work, but also the potential inherent in teaching for transformative work. For critical teaching, it means to struggle with students in understanding their resistance to forces acting upon their lives. It is the development of self and collective consciousness that can oppose the hegemony of the existing order, and begin to define and articulate our most desired human needs. Thus the ability of students to actively resist implies more than a change of consciousness. Patti Lather writes:

> The task of counter-hegemonic groups is the development of counter-institutions, ideologies, and cultures that provide an ethical alternative to the dominant hegemony, a lived experience of how the world can be different. (quoted in Weiler, 1988, p. 54)

A Way of Looking That Dances with Life

> A possible way of looking at things...gives the humanities their power to challenge the taken-for-granted, to move those who attend beyond their limited horizon. Maxine Green (1981, p. 302)

It is when we find our personally named human conditions unbearable that we can decide to act upon beliefs of what can be. In this action, freedom is taken as a movement leading towards a more compassionate existence. As such, freedom is relational, opening up the opportunities for greater human contact and reciprocity. The impetus towards this are painful feelings of alienation, powerlessness, and the vacuity felt from the decay of our moral and spiritual connections (Lerner, 1994). The "other side" that drives this movement are remembrances of past experiences of joy, happiness, touching, holding, closeness, community; those experiences that bring us in touch with the need for relationship in which love and understanding flourish. They produce the memories that can evoke our passion for life, one full of meaning, purpose, and joy (Marcuse, 1969). It is a movement grounded in the concrete dance with life, in which one remains in touch with human possibility. Maxine Greene (1981) writes concerning the link between critical thinking and possibility.

> Like Freire, I believe that the educator's efforts must coincide with those of the students to engage critical thinking and the quest for mutual humanization...there is an obligation, I think, on the part of all who educate to address themselves, as great artists do, to the freedom of their students, to make demands on them to form the pedagogy of their own liberation—to do so rigorously, passionately, and in good faith...there is possibility of transcendence, at least the transcendence of wide-awakeness, of being able to see. And to live with "eyes open" is something other than living submerged. (p. 298)

Greene's approach to the pedagogical process is in terms of conscious states of being, where students are called out of their submerged consciousness, their taken-for-granted world, and challenged to critically appropriate their own experience (Greene, 1990). In naming the existential dimensions of their lives, they gain insight into the very structures that form their ways of being. Reflection and understanding, in critical pedagogy, has as its purpose human freedom. Freedom, here, is a way of living, a praxis that has possibility as its project, giving meaning to one's life through a process of making connections. Praxis here is a bonding between the two faces of thinking and being; a "moral cementing" as thinking and feeling combine in an impassioned understanding of the human condition.

If thinking is a way of life, inextricable from how one lives, then freedom is synonymous with a way of thinking that is critical, creative, and visionary. David Purpel (1989) gives insight into the connections between the critical, creative, and moral aspects of education.

> Indeed, the essence of education can be seen as critical, in that its purpose is to help us to see, hear, and experience the world more clearly, more completely, and with more understanding.... Another vital aspect of the educational process is the development of creativity and imagination, which enable us not only to understand but to build, make, create, and re-create our world.... We are talking about a vision that can illuminate what we are doing and what we might achieve.... The questions of what our vision is and should be are in fact the most crucial and most basic questions that we face. (pp. 26-27)

Simply stated in terms of a critical pedagogy: the critical is turned toward the realities of living; the creative toward social transformation; and the moral toward the democratic principles of equality, social justice, freedom, and human dignity. The educational process then, becomes a paradigm for nourishing a critical and creative consciousness for the purpose of human freedom (Purpel, 1989).

Limitations of Critical Pedagogy

While critical pedagogy has offered me a perspective of incalculable value, on the philosophy of education and teaching, I've come to view the philosophy as having serious shortcomings. None of these is more apparent than the way it, as a discourse, has continued to speak in terms of mind/body dualism. I argue throughout this book that any approach committed to human liberation must seriously address the body as a site for both oppression and liberation. Recognizing the body, as well as the mind, as a cultural-historical construction illustrates the necessity for developing a critical discourse that expands our bodily understandings of human existence. Critical pedagogy, as an emancipatory philosophy, emphasizes a curriculum structured around students' experiences as a way of understanding the formation of one's identity. Yet, to understand this process we must also ask how the body absorbs and constructs particular ways of being as a vehicle for this socialization. Critical social theory has given us a framework that conceptualizes the relationship between being and consciousness—helping us to understand that not only does consciousness affect being, but being affects consciousness; how we think affects how we live, and conversely how we live affects how we think. Here thinking and being are in continual interplay. To a great extent, however, this ideological or dominant consciousness has been examined and understood in terms of the disembodied consciousness of the mind. The body, as the physical reflection of the culture in which one lives, has only more recently become part of the postmodern and feminist discourse. In terms of critical pedagogy, only recently has the question of what it might mean to take the body seriously been raised. Often when we talk about the body, it is in a highly abstract way. What is typically unexplored is the way the dominant culture is embodied and "lived out" in the individual subject. Indeed a great deal of my educational work has been, precisely, to "unpack" the forms of embodied culture with my students. "The human drama," writes Morris Berman; "is first and foremost a somatic one" (1989, p. 108) or as Emily Martin (1989 p. 15) might suggest for understanding human history, "at the level of the social whole, at the level of 'person,' and at the level of body."

It might seem a somewhat strange phenomenon, at this time of extraordinary questioning of paradigms and "regimes of truth," that it is necessary to restate the argument against the mind/body dualism in a discussion of critical social science and philosophy. Yet, our own scientifically-based model for understanding ourselves and our world has produced a methodology that continues to ensnare us in an acceptance of a language of separations and abstractions. This situation has not gone unnoticed. As Terry Eagleton (1996) notes, with insight and humor:

> The postmodern subject, unlike its Cartesian ancestor, is one whose
> body is integral to its identity. Indeed from Bakhtin to the Body Shop,
> Lyotard to leotards, the body has become one of the most recurrent
> preoccupations of postmodern thought. Mangled members, torment-
> ed torsos, bodies emblazoned or incarcerated, disciplined or desirous:
> the bookshops are strewn with such phenomena.... (p. 69)

In other words, there has been an extraordinary upsurge of interest among critical theorists in the question of the body. This has
reflected the strong critique of understanding and truth that
appear to emerge from objective, that is unsituated, human
thought and reason. Both among feminist and postmodern writers, there has been a determined attempt to see all knowledge as
emerging from human beings situated in very particular places,
cultures, languages, and histories. Nobody speaks or knows with
a God's-eye view. This assertion of situatedness can be seen as a
form of materialist philosophy, which starts, not with modes of
production, but with the body itself—the ultimate material presence in the world. I will, in succeeding chapters, return to this
postmodern turn of discourse. Let me say here, however, that
while this attention to the body has given great impetus to my
own work, it too is found wanting. Surprisingly, while we have
come to see just how much culture and language inscribe the
body, indeed construct it, there is still a relative lack of attention
and understanding of what this might mean for a pedagogy concerned with human emancipation and social change. Also, postmodern's antagonism towards notions of human agency has left
the body, paradoxically, in a peculiarly objectified state. I will
return to this in my final chapter of the book. Nonetheless, we
must take very seriously all that has been learned about the erasure of the body from our critical perspectives. It is also worth
reflecting on why there is now this embrace of the body among
intellectuals, especially those who are male. "Traditional, white,
western male philosophers," suggests Frigga Haug (1987, p. 28),
"are beginning all of a sudden to identify with the animalistic
body, perceiving their human identity threatened by the decision-
making process of the computer." She argues that our previous

conceptual framework, (which in its abstractions allowed for a mind/body separation, and further placed the 'mind' as the master of knowledge), has come under theoretical suspicion in its inability to provide a theory for understanding our human condition.

Under the influence of universally disruptive developments in the forces of production, the mode of domination articulated to the division of labour finds itself in a process of constant (and, currently, chaotic) reconstruction. Whereas previously it was the 'mind' that was to gain mastery both over body and nature, it is now the body that is to be saved from the ravages of the scientific and technical revolution.... The fact that the dualisms of body and mind, together with the division of labour between head and hand, have themselves been laid open to debate, can clearly be traced to their incapacity to explain the world as it is today. (p. 28)

The question of the mind/body dualism continues to be a terrain of compartmentalized investigation. The body has been divided into regions of biology, physiology, and kinesthetics all attempting to explain the functions of "body" in abstracted language. There is also the language of psychology, which discusses the body as an access to emotions for the mind to rationally sort out and take control of. The emphasis being on the individual gaining self-awareness and self-control. What is left out in these theories is the notion of a body/subject as a positioned social being. The consequence of this absence is that the experiences of the person come to be explained in highly individualistic terms (e.g., "You can learn how to control your stress."). Such statements give us the illusion that we're in control of our lives, but they disregard the social context in which our bodies are situated. We can come to better understand how to control our stress levels through internal relaxation processes, but we cannot begin to understand what induces the stress without consciously locating the existential realities of people in their everyday life as social beings. It becomes clear that without a particular kind of critical language that situates the body/subject in its social context, we continue to speak, in dualistic ways, of mind and body, individual and society. The absence of a dialectical reflective language that attempts to make these connections results in an inability to fully express and understand our lives, and therefore, to transform the conditions we live.

Fragmentation of understanding leads to abstraction of the self from its world situation, and from its embeddedness in social relations. Haug (1987, p. 64) writes, "Contrary to reputation, our everyday language is more than a little abstract: it suppresses the concreteness of feelings, thoughts, and experiences, speaking of them only from a distance." The way language is used directs our behavior. Language itself is taken to be reality, signs are as they appear. Therefore, language is the material through which we live, understand, and name our world. It begins in our earliest schooling. We learn to write about the facts of the world rather than about the lives that create it. We neither express the feelings we experience, nor do we have any means for reflecting on, or understanding them. Haug (1987) states, "We simply reproduce the perceptions we have heard spoken by others, from whose experience they are as equally far removed" (p. 65). This relationship between ideology and language is the overriding factor for instilling values as it structures behavior. Our relationship to language becomes strangely artificial as we learn to explain our world as if we exist outside of it.

Language without a Body

As critical educators have immersed themselves in exposing the relationships between the dominant ideology and the corresponding educational system, they have fallen into their own ideological trap. The concentrated effort in critical pedagogy to make explicit the relationship of power to the dominant form of knowledge often ignores body knowledge. Laurie McDade (1987) writes that knowing in the mind does not lie dormant, separate from the knowing of the heart and of the body.

> Everyday moments of teaching at school in communities, then, are personal, pedagogical, and political acts incorporating mind and bodies of subjects, as knowers and as learners. When we are at our best

as teachers we are capable of speaking to each of these ways of knowing ourselves and our students. And we may override precedents in
the educational project that value the knowing mind and deny the
knowing of the heart and body. Students, the partners in this enterprise of knowing, are whole people with ideas, with emotions, and
with sensations. If we, as teachers, 'are to arouse passions now and
then' (Greene, 1986, p. 441) the project must not be confined to a
knowing only of the mind. It must also address and interrogate what
we think we know of the heart and of the body. (pp. 58-59)

Any serious attempt to construct theories for understanding the
relationship between the individual and society must bridge the
gap between theory and experience, mind and body, and the rational and the sensual. We must question how we become "some-
body," if we are to outline strategies for liberation. This leads us
to examine how we have unconsciously accepted particular interpretations of the world, and how particular patterns of 'normali-
ty' have been drilled into us. The aim is to identify the ways in
which our consciousness becomes ideologized, and in so doing,
we begin to define and determine our relationship to other human
beings and to the larger world (Haug, 1987). To do so in bodily
terms is to reinterpret those taken-for-granted aspects of our lives
with an intention of investigating: (1) the ways in which bodily
activities are organized; (2) the ways in which the body itself and
the feelings in and around it have arisen historically; and (3) the
ways in which this relates to our insertion into society as a whole.

Guiding this investigation are two processes. The first is an
inquiry into our "body memories." Secondly, these memories are
given meaning by relating them to situations in which we volun-
tarily submit to our own subordination, or those in which we
develop forms of lived resistance. This decoding process
becomes the written signs of the relations within which subjectivity is formed. Critical social theorist Brian Fay (1987) tells us:

Put starkly, since the problem is not in people's minds nor dependent
on what goes on in them, then giving them insights into who they are,
raising their consciousness by altering their self-conceptions and
thereby altering their beliefs and values, is likely to be insufficient.

*Embodied repression calls for a strategy of liberation richer than
envisioned...* (p. 52) (Italics mine)

"Embodiment" refers to the process by which the body becomes
a vehicle for socialization. Fay argues (p. 146) that learning is not
simply a cognitive process, but also a somatic one in which the
"oppression leaves its traces not just in people's minds but in
their muscles and skeletons as well." In Peter McLaren's work in
critical pedagogy he speaks of "embodiment" defined as "the terrain of flesh where ideological social structures are inscribed."
McDade's, Fay's, and McLaren's work reflects an important
struggle for finding language that questions, understands, and
apprehends the unspoken knowledge of our bodies.

In a similar vein, Don Johnson (1983) vividly captures how,
through schooling, the physical bodies of students are patterned
to fit our social and economic structures. He argues that education is primarily designed to train docile citizens and workers and
this is partially achieved through forming bodily behavior. He
speaks of the unspoken inferences of a particular ordering of
"body knowledge," which becomes instilled within our bodies as
behaviors that lead to success.

> Bodily patterns of fatigue, hunger, and excitement are brought into
> alignment with the externally determined rhythm of the school day.
> Idiosyncratic behavior is generally punished, either physically, in the
> case of students who are too loud or restless, or through poor grades,
> in the case of those who don't express themselves 'correctly.' Industry
> is the principal beneficiary of these corporeal disciplines. Schools
> train people in the bodily patterns that most jobs require. The organic
> rhythms of the body are geared to meet the needs of the standardized
> working day, beginning and ending at certain hours, with carefully
> specified breaks for food, toilet, and rest. (p. 37)

McLaren (1988b) critiques education for insufficiently recognizing its own power to construct students' subjectivities by teaching us how to think about our bodies and how to experience our
bodies. He ascribes to language a powerful constitutive influence
in shaping the body/subject.

> The problem with schools is not that they ignore bodies, their plea-
> sures, and the suffering of the flesh (although admittedly this is part
> of the problem) but that they undervalue language and representation
> as a constitutive factor in the shaping of the body/subject as the bear-
> er of meaning, history, race, and gender. (p. 62)

We remain ignorant of the ideological use of language imposed upon the body, which speaks directly to the forming of subjectivity. This ignorance or lack of awareness of how our everyday language is packed with preconceived values and meanings becomes the obstacle in understanding the power concealed within language. Haug (1987, p. 63) writes, "Language can serve as either a prison house, or as the material for liberation." Not only does ignorance block possibilities for liberation, but the lack of an adequate language to bring to consciousness our "embodied" selves hinders the articulation of our experiences in theoretical terms. The project of liberation is once again thwarted in this disjunction between experience and language. The dominant discourse surrounds the attempt of liberatory actions and contains them within its ideological net—one that excises feelings and bodies in all of their torment. Ana Maria Araujo Freire wrote passionately in the afterword of Paulo Freire's *Pedagogy of Hope* (1994).

> I am fed up with bans and prohibitions: bans on the body, which pro-
> duce, generation after generation, not only Brazilian illiteracy
> (according to the thesis I maintain), but an *ideology* of ban on the
> body, which gives us our "street children," our misery and hunger, our
> unemployment and prostitution, and, under military dictatorship, the
> exile and death of countless Brazilians. (Freire, 1994, p. 204)

She notes too, the ban on Paulo Freire's body (along with his ideas), which was forbidden, for fifteen long years, in Brazil.

The body is not to be understood as an abstract object, it is not other. It is real. It is by definition an I with that which is more than the mind and more than the physical body. It is not a dualistic split or even multiple splits. It is the presence of all that we know, housed in stories of meaning.

Stanley Keleman (1981), suggested that the education of the body occurs in two specific ways. One is direct somatic learning in which the body becomes the receptor for behavioral influences addressed through language and physical environments (i.e., "Sit still"; "Face front"; "Don't touch anyone or anything"; "Keep your legs together"; "Stand tall"). And the second process is indirect somatic learning, noted, for example, in educational institutions, when the student learns acceptable ways of being particular to his or her culture by taking on roles (e.g. the role of mastery: "Don't cry"; "Swallow your anger"; "Keep a stiff upper lip"; of occupation: "How much schooling have you had?"; "What's your earning capacity?"; and, that of sexuality: "Girls don't argue"; "Boys don't cry"). To be concerned with the shaping of the body/subject is to remember as Keleman (1981, p. 13) writes, "The body you have is the body you live." Our feelings and responsiveness shape our lives. We form our bodily selves as we shape our own reality. Our bodily living shapes our existence. Thus, for example, he suggests:

> In the name of Knowledge we dampen and channel aliveness. Our current system of education creates spasms. We cramp our children's bodies so that we can form their minds. The school system institutes a social contract between the kids and the teachers, and between the kids and adult authorities in general. And the model is a contraction model. Learning becomes painful. Learning becomes a chore that requires discipline. (p. 128)

The forming of our being grows out of our experiences. Experiences are perceived in coordination between our minds and bodies—that which forms our being. This forming is the historically situated, culturally inscribed "reality" in which we live. Morris Berman (1989) gives a lived example of the educational spasm of which Keleman speaks of.

> I was born and raised in upstate New York. During my high school years, we were required, as part of the history sequence of our education, to spend time learning about local and regional history. Our textbook had a chapter about the Colonial period, another about the defeat

of the Iroquois, still another about the building of the Erie Canal, as well as ones on the rise of the steel and textile industries. For all I remember, there may even have been chapters on working-class movements, strikes, the formation of labor unions, possibly something on the life of Emma Goldman (though I doubt it). (pp. 107-108)

That I don't remember is largely the point here. It was all crushingly boring; it seemed to have little relevance to anything that really mattered, to me or any of the other students forced to study this material.... Chemistry and Latin were no different from history, even though history was supposedly about "real life." Yet none of us were deceived about what actually constituted real life. Real life was your awkwardness in front of the opposite sex, your relations with your peers, your struggle to cope with what went on in your family...(what resonates with what is familiar to you). In a word, your emotions, or more broadly, your "spiritual" and psychic life. *These things are what your real life is about; they reflect the things that matter most to you, for they are experienced in the body.* (pp. 107-108) (Italics mine)

Critical educators need to understand that the process of liberation requires that the body be situated linguistically, and therefore discursively, in the sociohistorical context. To *write the body* is to understand that "the voice is the body" (p. 58), representing the incorporation of the social into the corporeal. Therefore, it is within this specific context that body/subjects are able to recognize the set of connections necessary "to make sense" of their lives, and thereby begin to consciously define both their own subjugation and possibilities for liberation.

A language that emerges from our bodily living speaks of a kind of rationality distinct from one that is *intellectually* rooted. It demands that we listen to our bodies, feel our emotions, release our passions, and reunite our critical powers of thinking with our feelings in hopes of a fuller humanity. As stated earlier, even in our critical discourse we continue to speak in terms of a rational-mind orientation. In rational thinking, students are encouraged to see beyond the surface of the ideology in which they live, ask for justifications, seek alternatives, and be critical of their own ideas, as well as others. Missing in the text is literacy of embodied knowledge, which is essential to adequately address contemporary issues such as colonization, difference, identity, affects of technology and media, gender, commodification, and capitalism (Gutierrez & McLaren in Kanpol & McLaren, 1995). All of this suggests the need to "embody the discourse" of critical pedagogy. Critical awareness must enter new territories in order to address the overriding emphasis in institutions of education on valuing the knowing mind, which continually denies the knowing of the heart and of the body. What is to be exposed is what remains absent, silent, and un-named, revealing the relationship between language and ideology, and specifically the failure to adequately name the way we live, as embodied beings.

References

Bartky, S. (1990). *Feminity and domination*. New York: Routledge.

Berman, M. (1989). *Coming to our senses: Body and spirit in the hidden history of the west*. New York: Simon & Schuster.

Brosio, R. (1994). *A radical democratic critique of capitalist education*. New York: Peter Lang.

Bruss, N., & Macedol, D. (1985). Toward a pedagogy of the question: Conversations with Paulo Freire. *Journal of Education*, 167(2), 7-22.

Eagleton, T. (1996). *The illusions of postmodernism*. Oxford: Blackwell.

Fay, B. (1987). *Critical social science*. New York: Cornell University.

Foucault, M. (1977). *Discipline and punishment* (A. Sheridan, Trans.). New York: Pantheon Books.

Freire, P. (1994). *A pedagogy of hope: Reliving pedagogy of the oppressed*. New York: Continuum.

Freire, P. (1988). *Pedagogy of the oppressed*. New York: Continuum.

Giroux, H. (1985). Critical pedagogy, cultural politics and the discourse of experience. *Journal of Education*, 167(2), 22-41.

Giroux, H.A., & Simon, R.I. (1988). Schooling, popular culture, and a pedagogy of possibility. *Journal of Education*, 170(1), 9-26.

Greene, M. (1986). In search of a critical pedagogy. *Harvard Educational Review*, 56(4), 427- 441.

Greene, M. (1990, Spring). Multiple voices and multiple realities: A re-viewing of educational foundations. *Educational Foundations*, 5-19.

Greene, M. (1981). The humanities and emancipatory possibility. *Journal of Education*, 163(4), 287-305.

Hammer, R., & McLaren, P. (1989). Critical pedagogy and the postmodern challenge. *Educational Foundations*, 3(3), 29-62.

Haug, F. (1987). *Female sexualization*. London: Verso.

Heidegger, M. (1968). *What is called thinking* (F. Wieck, & J. Gray, Trans.). New York: Harper & Row.

Heidegger, M. (1962). *Being and time* (J. Macquarrier, & E. Robinson, Trans.). New York: Harper & Row.

Johnson, D. (1983). *Body*. Boston: Beacon Press.

Kanpol. B. (1994). *Critical pedagogy: An introduction*. Connecticut: Bergin & Garvey.

Kanpol, B. & McLaren, P. (Eds.). (1995). *Critical multiculturalism: Uncommon voices in a common struggle*. Connecticut: Bergin & Garvey:

Keleman, S. (1981). *Your body speaks its mind*. Berkeley: Center Press.

Kundera, M. (1991). *Immortality*. New York: Harper Collins.

Lerner, M. (1994). *Jewish renewal: A path to healing and transformation*. New York: Putnam's Sons.

Marcuse, H. (1969). *Essays on liberation*. Boston: Beacon Press.

Martin. E. (1989). *The woman in the body: A cultural analysis of reproduction*. Boston: Beacon Press.

McDade, L. (1987). Sex, pregnancy, and schooling: Obstacles to a critical teaching of the body. *Journal of Education*, 169(3), 58-79.

McLaren, P. (1989). *Life in schools*. New York: Longman.

McLaren, P. (1988b). Broken dreams, false promises, and the decline of public schooling. *Journal of Education*, 170(1), 41-65.

McLaren, P. (1988b). Schooling the postmodern body: Critical pedagogy and the politics of enfleshment. *Journal of Education,* 170(3), 53-83.

Middleton, S. (1993). *Educating feminists.* New York: Columbia University Teacher's College Press.

Nieto. S. (1996). *Affirming diversity.* New York: Longman.

Purpel, David E. (1989). *The moral and spiritual crisis in education.* Massachusetts: Bergin & Garvey.

Purpel, D. E. & Shapiro, S. (1995). *Beyond liberation and excellence.* Connecticut: Bergin & Garvey

Seidel, G. (1964). *Martin Heidegger and the pre-Socratics.* Lincoln: University of Nebraska Press.

Shapiro, H. S. (1989). Curriculum alternatives in a survivalist culture: Basic skills and the "minimal self." *New Education,* 8(2), 3-14.

Simon, R. (1987). Empowerment as a pedagogy of possibility. *Language Arts,* 64(4), 370.

Weiler, K. (1988). *Women teaching for change.* Massachusetts: Bergin & Garvey.

West, C. (1988). Interview by Anders Stephanson. In A. Ross (Ed.), *Universal abandon* (pp. 269-288). Minneapolis: University of Minnesota Press.

Young-Bruehl, E. (1982). *Hannah Arendt: For the love of the world.* London: Yale University Press.

CHAPTER TWO

The Body and Knowledge: Towards Relational Understanding

This chapter investigates the epistemological subordination of a concrete language of the body-experience to one that is abstracted from the lived social world. The argument develops through a description of separations of the rational being from the sensual one. These are examined through the philosophical, theological and sociological discourses that have historically shaped our contemporary ways of thinking, and of being.

My interest is to give insight to the ways in which the subordination and denial of body knowledge, or of sensate lived experience, informs the dominant ways in which we think, believe, and value. The particular discourse in which these are represented, I argue, is one, that disconnects us from that which is felt and experienced, rather than observed and made visible. The order of the "rational" over the "irrational" brings to question, in this chapter, the relationship between reason and sensing in forming knowledge. In the attempt to reveal the issues involved in "thinking about thinking," there is the disclosure of a discourse that alienates us from our own abilities to acknowledge and become responsible for our understanding, to recognize the relational and dialectical nature of ourselves and our bodies as the mediators of all knowledge.

In the first section, "Knowledge as the Dialectic of Mind and Body," I focus on the interpenetration of mind and body as the means through which we come to understand our world. My attempt is to illuminate the body as that which mediates and holds in memory the experiences of our lives, and in so doing, create a critical discourse for the body. Writing in this section is an inter-weaving and synthesis of theories and themes that reoccur throughout this chapter.

The second section, "Historical and Philosophical Origins of the Problem," focuses upon how the dominant paradigm of rationalistic thinking grew out of the duality of mind and body, and how this duality has been destructive to relational and experiential knowing. The exploration of the separation of being and thinking is drawn from the work of Martin Heidegger in which he establishes how early philosophical traditions led to the epistemological exclusion of the body.

In the third section, "Body and Society: An Inseparable Identity," questions concerning how the dominant paradigm of knowing has affected our values and notions of morality are examined through the work of Michel Foucault, Brian Turner's work on sociology of the body, Brian Fay's work in critical theory, and Frigga Haugg's feminist work. Using these authors I focus upon the cultural polarities of male reason and female passion, and how these are expressed in separation of the public and private domains within society. What I wish to make clear in this section is the way in which the body is situated by, and within, relationships of power. Through consideration of the ideological subjugation of the body/private/female in patriarchal discourse, I attempt to demonstrate issues of power and dominance that permeate all of our social relations.

Knowledge as the Dialectic of Mind and Body

To engage in the dialectic of self and society one must first engage in, as John Berger (1982) calls it, "Another Way of Telling" in which appearances of the culture are treated as signs addressed to the living. The appearance of what we see and accept as knowledge is only half the language. To think, feel, or remember goes beyond surface descriptions. Embedded within perceptions and interpretations are personal experiences understood through a hegemonic consciousness that suspends us in the contradictions between a dominant and a resistant consciousness. From this space between domination and resistance is where meaning is found, securing the living body as the material that holds both. Ideas do not exist somewhere outside of this living material. What we know is at all times attached to bodily knowing, whether as tacit knowing or as conscious knowing. What we know speaks with and to our bodily memories of living. Both mind and body mingle together in a continuous informational stream creating the interpretations we call knowledge. As such, we experience our interpretations as reality. This continual forming of ourselves gives rise to philosophies, dogmas, and other image-systems that, by stereotyping us, assure us a sense of perpetual identity (Keleman, 1981). This forming is a creative process and can be either conscious or unconscious. Marion Woodman (1985) distinguishes the inseparability of the two.

> Ultimately, conscious and unconscious are one. *The conscious purpose is* not simply to reproduce or perpetuate, but *to know* [italics added]. It is the difference between unconscious creation and conscious creation. (p. 119)

Woodman accentuates the relationship between consciousness and knowledge as one that requires a critical contextualization. To be ignorant of the dominant consciousness, which forms our knowledge systems, is to limit our human potential to reproducing and perpetuating our current condition. Without awareness of the relationship between critical thinking and the ways in which we live our everyday lives, we remain, to a large degree, in a state of unconscious creation. This common tendency can be traced back to philosophical traditions when the separation between mind and body, being and thinking occurred. (I will return to this discussion later in the chapter.)

Contrary to what has been the dominant tendency in European philosophies of thinking, Heidegger reattaches thinking to being. He turns us away from thinking as a kind of gathering of knowledge that can be separated from that which gathers. Thinking, he argues, is to be learned; and to learn is to address oneself to the relatedness between oneself (as subject) and the world within which one is living—being-in-the-world. Only then can understanding of being begin.

Touching is the extension of human consciousness; sensing through the hand materializes the life-world. Language is the abstraction of touch. It represents how we think and makes materially present the consciousness with which we live. Not only an act of creation, but also one that provides us with ontological security, a physical reassurance (Berman, 1989, p. 44). "All the work of the hand is rooted in thinking," writes Heidegger. "And only when man speaks, does he think" (1968, p. 16). I take the meaning of Heidegger's statement critically (aware of the use of "man" rather than human) as it speaks again to a phase of understanding as one that is rational; but what I also understand is the strong relationship between thinking (even if uncritically) and the creating of our realities. And further, that in the act of articulation of one's understandings and desires can we cast reflexivity upon thinking. Only when we begin to hear the impoverished nature of our rational language and begin to see the destructive work of our hands, can we begin to understand the power of human touch. Our impoverished thinking displays itself in the social injustices and inequalities, continually and materially exposed, in the "fleshless" bodies of starving children; in the glazed-over eyes of humans addicted to narcotizing their senses to protect themselves from the harsh realities of life; and in bodies that simply wear out in the struggle for survival. John Berger (1984, p. 33) defines our human response to the death of life as he writes, "What we mourn for in the dead is the loss of their hopes." As caring and concerned human beings we ask, "What is this language that has perverted our humanity?" We look out and see that the inscriptions of our hands are left everywhere.

The work of John Berger and others, such as Andrea Dworkin, suggests that there is nothing between touching and not touching. Both create a conduit from the past into the future. Postmodern thinkers such as Richard Rorty and Jacques Derrida have theorized the relationship between language and shaping of our life-world, arguing that our world exists as we have, and continue to name it. Every life encounters the human touch. What it carries is our fingerprints. The unheard and unspoken words of children, minorities, women, blacks, jobless, homeless, and "others" are turned inward to echo inside their own "life bodies."

Historical and Philosophical Origins of the Problem

"Reason," Heidegger argues (1968), "is the perception of what is, which always means also what can be and ought to be" (p. 41). It is this understanding of reason that concerns itself with possibility grounded in critical understanding and contextualized through reflection upon concrete existence. Possibility here retains within it an understanding of both "what is" and "what is not"—"what is missing" and "what is desired." Implied is a way of thinking that is anchored in one's everyday life and made sense of through the process of giving meaning to sensate-lived experiences. Through a process of "sensual reasoning" one becomes actively engaged in refusing the mind and body separation. Reasoning as an ability to critically situate oneself in an historical and social grounding runs in opposition to modern societies that have adopted a paradigmatic model of thinking based in abstraction and rationality. Audre Lorde (Weiler, 1991) questions the depth of any critical understanding that is not rooted in the examination of what one has experienced and lived in concrete ways, in one's own body; it calls for a materialistic conception of experience. Inherent in many feminist critiques of the "mind-oriented," scientific paradigm for understanding the world is the interrogation of any paradigmic view that does not value feeling, lived experience (as explored through memory) as something in process, and the tensions and complexities contained in the validation of difference (p. 470). As Adrienne Rich points out: "To think like a woman in a man's world means...remembering that every mind resides in a body; remaining accountable to the female bodies in which we live; constantly retesting given hypotheses against lived experience" (Weiler, p. 465). What became clear through early feminist work was the inseparability of body knowledge and issues of power and politics. And more recently with deconstructionist postmodernism, even though it stands against disembodied knowledge, it also dislodges the body from any particular location and therefore, any possibility for unity or stability of identity (having multiple embodiments, being nowhere and everywhere). This paradigm, rather than placing the body (as in the Cartesian view) in the position in which it needs to be transcended to achieve an objective-true view undistorted from human perspective, places the body nowhere. As Susan Bordo (1990) asserts: "If the body is a metaphor for our locatedness in space and time and thus for the finitude of human perception and knowledge, then the postmodern body is no body at all" (p. 145). This erasure of the body in deconstructionism will be returned to in the final chapter, but now I will return to the earlier beginnings of the story of the mind as understood in relationship to its separation from the body.

The sensual body has been historically bound by the domination of a idealist tradition that, since Plato, placed the mind over body, and ideas over the senses (Seidel, 1964). In this the body came to be understood biologically or physically, rather than existentially. Another crucial dimension in the history of the separation of mind from body is Christian theology, which pointed its finger at the body as something that housed evil desires and passions, and therefore needed to be held under the laws of the rational (and more Godly) mind. The historical verdict was a "guilty and sinful body," and an oppressive discourse of sacrifice, acceptance of suffering, humility, and meekness (Welch, 1985, p. 15). And feminist scholarship has long claimed the body as a site for emancipatory struggle and ontological knowing. What is being suggested here is the early existential philosophical changes that emerged in Heidegger's work.

Heidegger's concept of reason that is constituted through thinking and being (concrete existence), calls into question the historical separation of mind and body, and the subordination of the body from epistemological discussion.

> Under the predominance of rationalism, the cognitive function of sensuousness has been constantly minimized. Sensuousness retained (in Western traditional thought) a measure of philosophical dignity in a subordinate epistemological position; those of its processes that did

not fit into the rationalistic epistemology; that is those that went beyond the passive perception of data—become homeless. Foremost among these homeless content and values were those of imagination: free, creative, or reproduction intuition of objects which are not directly 'given'. (Marcuse, 1969: 180)

This quote from Marcuse, one of Heidegger's most prominent students, reminds us of the relationship between the elevated position of the mind in a rationalistic model of knowing and the diminishing one of the body. Concerns for what is left out in this mode of thinking shift the conversation to examine what Marcuse names as "the homeless" values—those that carry no epistemological weight, those that cannot be captured under the scientific lens. One such "homeless" value is human imagination—that which embeds creativity and change, and the contemplation of human possibility. The possibility for imagination is vital to a pedagogy of liberation in that imagination coexists with a sense of possibility of transformation.

This philosophical separation of being and thinking, or Physis and Logos, was Heidegger's avenue for studying the origination of modern Western philosophy. Seidel (1964) details Heidegger's description of this separation as "the most decisive factor for the western tradition of philosophy" (p. 58).

I will briefly sketch how the dominant paradigm in thinking has separated thinking and being, mind and body, in an attempt to label "what is" as a kind of observable factual truth. My attempt is to examine, through Heidegger's work, the early divisions in philosophical thinking that have led us to value rational knowing over experiential knowing. There are several ways of identifying and addressing the problems that arise in the separation and devaluation of experiential or body knowledge. I have chosen to present my argument in terms of "choosing life"—that is, a reflexive awareness of existence as opposed to unconscious acceptance of the pre-existing world into which one is born. This discourse becomes the focal point for understanding how our bodily existence—imprinted with the existential knowledge of our concrete lives—has been virtually left out of the domain of theoretical thinking. More directly my concern is the dissonance between our dominant ways of thinking and the lives we live.

Appearance vs. Existence

The forgetting of "being" occurred, according to Heidegger, when philosophers rooted being in the "thingliness of things"— that is, when ontological questions turned from "being of things" to appearance of the "substance of things" (Seidel, 1964). This transition was from the "to be" of a thing to the "is" of a thing. The "to be" incorporates the issue of time, which carries both the past and the future. With this is the acknowledgment of humankind as the carrier of time, (rather than time existing outside of humanity), and allowance for the possibility of change to occur both in what we have named as history and what is possible for the future. Further, what is disclosed is that history is created by being, carried into the present as life, and projected into the future from the present as possibility. History in this sense does not exist somewhere outside of human creation, but is continuously being created, re-created, and projected by and through the historical stories we live. Humankind is co-creator with physical nature in life, and is responsible for both life and world.

This recognition of humanity creating its own history speaks to a historical sensibility that accepts the possibility of human agency for changing the history we live. The "to be" places the body in the center as a preceptor of life. It is with the body that one connects existence with a desire for change. Participation of the sensing, feeling, perceptive body is required to make sense of one's everyday life. Conceptualization is not enough for change. The order of the rational-irrational is shattered in the continuous exchange between reason and sensing. (For most Americans, their idea of the "American dream" is drastically different from the lives that are lived in bodies that are fatigued, stressed, and pushed to make the dream come true.) Awareness of the perceptive, sensual body presents a dilemma in the delineation of reality for a society that has relinquished "the living body" to abstract reason.

"To be" conveys movement in time—something as becoming, in a state of motion, in a process of changing. "To be" is antithetical to "is," which exists in stasis in the present. Inherent in the transition from "to be" to "is" is the loss of human time—life. What is left are "facts" of the present understood as the actual presence of something as it can be observed, unhindered by its sociohistorical context. Failing to acknowledge the difference sets up a paradigm for knowing that emphasizes the "observing eye" over the "telling body." Stories of life are restricted to facts which can be statistically read and analyzed to reveal some universal standards applicable to human life. Sharon Welch (1985, p. 38) clarifies two limitations when the primary task of academics becomes the disclosure of universal kinds of knowledge and their correlation with the ontological structure of existence. First, such an ontological analysis brackets the concrete specificity of historical concerns; and second, the experiences of certain groups of people are excluded from the analysis. Abstraction and exclusion break down relational understanding and bleed history dry, leaving the scars of separation.

Histories that emphasize the narrative of human suffering can lead to a disclosure of the denial of particular histories, including those of blacks, native Americans, women, and others marginalized in the dominant male Euro-centric culture. The pretension that one's class, race, and/or sex speaks for all of humanity reveals the victors in the struggle over whose history is told and whose history is projected into the future. More dangerous is when that pretension is taken to its full extreme, as in the case of the Nazis' genocide of six million Jews. Robert Lifton in his writings concerning "The Genocidal Mentality" (1990) states:

> Somewhere in the intellectual history of the West there developed the wrongheaded idea that mind and heart are antagonists, that scholarship must be divested of emotion, that spiritual journeys must avoid intellectual concerns. (p. 29)

The expressed values in Lifton's quote can be noted as he reveals the intellectual detachment from spiritual or moral concerns. Here values are restricted to a scientific definition where values comes to be the property of something separated from human emotion, feeling, and connection. Yet moral questions can only be asked in terms of relationships, as we can only ask moral questions in context.

The preoccupation of Physis with "the present" produced a truth rooted in an empirical paradigm (Seidel, 1964). The fate of being, as Heidegger suggests (in Seidel), was given over to the notion of "things are as they appear," particulary in the philosophy of Plato. Being, at this time, was segregated from that which could be disclosed about itself in the act of presencing. The objectified thing became the thing to be known, rather than valued as something that could tell us about human beings and their relationship to the world. On the contrary, relevant questions concerning the nature of being human as such, the possibility of meaning, and the structures of being that underlie particular manifestations of human life, were disregarded by those positioned by society as "truth-givers"—either the religious or the scientific. The importance of this lies in the change in the location of truth; whereas, in the latter sensibility truth is revealed in the uncovering of the relationship between subjects; in the former, truth is to stand alone outside of relational contamination, and therefore moral considerations.

The Greek notion of being as the "coming forth and staying around for awhile" held a twofold meaning: (1) what appears or emerges; and (2) what is permanent (Seidel, 1964, p. 34). This critical point is where Heidegger directs attention to the transformation of Western philosophical thinking. Before the abstraction, Logos and reason projected the concern for the complexity of relationships. That is to say, when humans look out into the world to discover or come to know something, what is revealed is not something directly about the object, but about being itself. It raises questions about who is doing the looking, what is chosen to be looked at and what is not, what questions are asked or omitted, and what the relationship between the subject and the object reveals about being human. In other words, the object (or objective knowing) cannot escape its involvement with the subject (or subjective knowing), since it is the subject that sees, names, and interprets from a specific location in human history. As such, this "assignment" or reference by being indicates wherein the human concern dwells (Heidegger, 1962). *Truth, then, is in the event of the relationship between subject and object.* To understand being is to understand the relationship between wo/man and her/his world.

In summarizing, relational understanding constitutes our "sight." It is always understood in terms of the totality of involvement between subject and object, and therefore locates understanding or "truth" in its sociohistorical context. Recaptured is a process that acknowledges the interdependence of personal experience, feeling, *and* theoretical knowledge. The abstracted-objectified "thing" is replaced by the relational context. And finally, the concern of knowledge is, once again, everyday existence—the life-world. *The investigation* is not to find the correctness of an idea or the knowledge of things, or as a declaration of something present before us. *It is rather one that is concerned with seeing something in its presence as constituted by both what has been and the possibilities of what can be. Meaning then is found in this process through a relocating of "truth" in being-in-the-world, and through a unification of being and thinking in an existential hermeneutic.*

Relational understanding means then that *knowledge is always grounded in bodily existence*, recognized as interpretive, and acknowledged as always being partial. Critical understanding of one's life and world means then to take seriously the connection that comes from the dialectic of mind and body, embodied existence and reasoned knowing.

Below I look more concretely at the situatedness of the body in culture. Here, too, I continue my attempt to develop and create a discourse of the body.

Body and Society: An Inseparable Identity

*A Dichotomy between a Static Language
and a Concrete Language of Existence*
When is a language finished? Do we see things as they are, and forever know them? What prevents language from being static? If I choose to name one thing something else, does the first cease

to exist? Do I know the power of the words that create my life as it is?

The dichotomy between a static or seamless language and a concrete-experiential language emerges when one tries to theorize a sociology of knowledge or consciousness. Without the body we cannot speak a concrete language of the transactions between the natural ordering of the world and the cultural ordering of the world. Brian Turner (1984) argues the inseparableness of the so-called natural world and the cultural world particular to the body.

> The body has physiological needs, in particular food, liquid, and sleep. The nature, content, and timing of these activities of eating, drinking, and sleeping are subject to symbolic interpretations and to massive social regulations. We can thus think of the body as an outer surface of interpretations and representations and an internal environment of structures and determinations. (pp. 39-40)

Second, Turner notes that the sociology of the body is political in that it concerns the struggle between the powerful and the powerless over the nature of desire. Examples of this can easily be seen in laws concerning abortion, illegitimacy, homosexuality, and prostitution, and more generally the regulation of sexual behavior.

Third, he argues the body lies at the center of political struggles in its "sexualization." He gives as an example a doctrine of patriarchal sovereignty enunciated in 1680.

> The king is the father over his kingdom; Adam was the father over nature and humanity; God is father over man. Patriarch then comes before the authority of law and is the source of all rights and obligations. Authority is thus transubstantiated through the bodies of kings just as it is transubstantiated through the body of fathers.

In this example, the body of man receives power and authority simply by virtue of being a particular kind of body.

And fourth, Turner states, the body and the self are not separate. If the self is realized in social relationships, the body is that physical presence that reacts externally and internally. An example is in blushing or flushing in reaction to social discomfort, and internally reacting with diseases and illnesses as expressions of the relationship between the body and the life-world. Both are considered to be deviant from "the norm" and become visibly present through the body.

There are some things that we know as experienced in our own lives. As socially-constructed beings, we blush as our bodies express embarrassment when what we have said or are unable to say indicates our ignorance in front of others. Our bodies stiffen from work situations that either create stress, or constrict movement into ritualistic patterns. Muscles contract in these situations, representing the restrictions of the self that may be needed to control one's anger, or to repress one's desires in order to fit into the structured norms of the workplace.

This socialization process between body and society is not simply the insertion of the body/subject into preexistent social and cultural formations; it also implies an affective investment on the part of the subject in relationship to a particular symbolic order. "Enfleshment" is a term used by critical theorists to convey a state of being where there is an unproblematic acceptance, appropriation, and identification of the body/subject with any such preexistent set of symbolic meanings. Yet, McLaren (1989) suggests though that the body does more than incorporate ideas, it also generates them. Ideas have a "social materiality" presented in forms of thinking and being; they are "enfleshed" in ideologies, and historical and cultural forms of subjectivity. Enfleshment is conceived here as the mutually-constitutive aspect of social structure and desire. Discourse is the materialization of those symbols in our social structures and in our bodies. McLaren (1988) writes:

> Discourses do not sit on the surface of the flesh nor float about in the formless ether of the mind but are enfolded into the very structures of our desire inasmuch as desire itself is formed by the anonymous historical rules of discourse.... Desire and its social determinations, its

cultural objects of desire, cannot be seen separately but must be
understood as mutually constitutive. (p. 61)

Desires can be considered as lacks, gaps, or needs felt to
complete our subjectivity. Forms of desire can be linked historically to "modes of production." McLaren (1988) notes that every
mode of production has a mode of desire. The term modes of
desire refers to the different ways in which desire is socially constructed (p. 63). These objects of desire are not created in a value-
free laboratory, but rather in conjunction with an economic structure that perpetuates itself by creating desires, and in return the
products to fulfill those desires. These desires come to be seen by
us as something needed to complete our subjectivity. For example, advertising is geared toward helping you to become a more
complete, more successful, more beautiful (and so on) person. In
an advertising strategy, a gap or lack is created, and then com-
municated to the buyer so that s/he has the possibility *to be* more
by having more. The gap between "what you are" and "what you
can be" becomes a desire, (whether it is to have a slimmer figure,
have a shinier kitchen floor, or have a faster car). This creates an
economy based on the production of desire and production of
desired objects. For example, capitalism engages in constructing
"buyable" substitutions for human desires, such as relationships
or security. Picture the advertisements in which beautiful women
are shown alongside cars. Directed toward men in this case, it is
suggested that in purchasing the car, the buyer is likely to attract
(in this car) beautiful women. McLaren (1988, p. 64) elaborates
on this subject's experience: "In this context, consumer needs are
often superimposed on the desires of the body so that the subject's intention to satisfy the body must make a detour through
exchange value; the response to the demands of the body is
deferred, for the visible aim of laboring is the wage (Brenkman,
1987, p. 182).
       My argument is that this kind of material substitution and
production of desire inhabits our flesh and consumes our
thoughts, placing our subjectivity under the power of those who
control production. Consumption-driven, we live the economic

nightmare of finding ourselves in a constant state of desire for the next consumer "fix." Desire and its social determinations cannot be separated in a critical analysis, but must be understood as mutually constitutive.

In the following section, I will continue to discuss the mobilization of desire in terms of the division between male reason and female passion. I begin by focusing on the objectification of the body.

The Culture of Anti-Body: Reason and the Suppression of Desire
Brian Turner's (1984) work on sociology and the body stresses the Western tradition of the mind-body dualism as influenced by religion and science. Western traditions of dualistic thinking—as the opposition between spirit and flesh—has its origins, he says, in Hellenized Christianity. Turner (1984) provides a historical description of the body's objectification in this opposition.

Private	Public
desire	reason
female	male
informal	formal
affectivity	neutrality
particularity	universality
diffusion	specificity
hedonism	asceticism
consumption	production

The body in Greek thought has been the focus of the struggle between form and desire (between Apollo and Dionysus). Christianity inherited this viewpoint, but darkened it by seeing the flesh as the symbol of the Fallen Man and irrational denial of God. In medieval times, the celebration of the body in festival and carnival came to be a political expression of popular dissent against the dominant literate tradition of the court and the urban centers of social control. Rabelais' confirmation of the primitive and popular language of the body in the tradition of the marketplace and carnival was thus an affront to the refinement expressed in 'official' literature. Within the sociology of the knowledge, therefore, it is possible to trace a secularization of the body in

which the body ceases to be the object of a sacred discourse of flesh
to an object within a medical discourse where the body is a machine
to be controlled by appropriate scientific regimens. (p. 36)

Derived from this tradition was "the body" as the seat of unrea-
son, passion, and desire. The flesh of our bodies became the symbol of moral corruption. So strongly was the threat of the flesh to
Christianity that it named the body as deviant to the correct order
of the world, and therefore the flesh had to be subdivided by disciplines, by "bodily order" (Turner, 1984).

Turner traces the shift away from eighteenth-century religious discourse concerning the body to the nineteenth-century
scientific discourse of the body. In the former, the body was seen
as a flesh full of passion and desire destructive to mankind,
which, therefore had to be controlled and disciplined. In the latter, the body became an object understood in mechanistic terms
to be controlled by appropriate scientific regimens. The shift was
from maintenance of a healthy body as a religious value, to concern for efficient quantification of the body. The result of this
change was a reification and objectification of the body that
became a focus of exact calculation. Such change may appear to
be liberatory in that it reduces the moral significance of the body,
yet, as argued by Adorno (*Dialectic of Enlightenment*, 1972), at
the same time there is an objectification of the body in the desire
to control all forms of nature. The notion of enlightenment opens
up the drive for objectification and control of nature, both inner
(i.e., the body) and outer.

The medical or scientific discourse creates a language that
speaks of the body in terms that measure its form, fragments it
into parts, and therefore divides up its desires and passions. This
division, argues Turner, is not a physiological fact but a cultural
construct, and therefore a political act that locates antisocial
behavior within the passionate, desirous body. Andrea Dworkin
(1987) situates the threat of the sensuous in the duality of mind
and body.

To be "reasonable" means to put oneself into a special, rarely happy relationship to the sensuous. "Be Reasonable" means, practically speaking, do not trust your impulses, do not listen to your body, learn control, starting with your own sensuousness. (p. 169)

Turner (1984) relates the political implications of the construction of these "anti-body" discourses, from Hellenized Christianity to the Age of Enlightenment, to the distribution of power in relationship to masculine and feminine traits. He takes us beyond oppression of the body in such discourses to the notion of the challenge presented to the social order by the female body. (I will return to this issue in the following chapter).

The contradiction between passion and reason...is also the vindication of authority which provides the root of social order and social solidarity...[argues] not simply that the body is culturally constructed in opposition to social authority, but specifically that the female body is the main challenge to continuity of property and power. The division between female passion and male reason is thus the cultural source of patriarchy. (p. 37)

Turner views the division between female passion and male reason as a spatial distribution between the public and private realm. The private space in modern society is characterized by intimacy and emotionality while the public space is characterized by formality, neutrality, and impersonality. Turner (p. 38) provides a schema that illustrates a spatial division between passions (in the private sphere) and reasons (in the public sphere).

The split between private life and labor, consumption and production, is a necessary social mechanism to alleviate the dissatisfactions arising from the frustration and boredom of work (Shapiro, 1990, p. 56). Shapiro argues that consumerism has developed as an ideal at the same time as the older religious belief in the work ethic declined. Work is no longer thought about in terms of creative production, but rather as a purely instrumental activity—a means rather than an end of human action. The repressive realm of consumption, notes Shapiro, still needs to be distinguished from the equally coercive realm of production.

> While the latter contains the ascetic moment of bourgeois culture (the
> work ethic, impulse restraint, duty, delayed gratification), consump-
> tion, with its demand for happiness and self-fulfillment contains a
> critical element in its focus. Consumption...still means a protest
> against asceticism of traditional bourgeois culture. (1990, p. 55)

In this division as noted by Turner and Shapiro, life is divided into two realms. In the public world of production, there is
work as the social struggle for existence and the transformation of
nature. In the private realm is the personal domain of consumption—leisure and human fulfillment, and the quest for meaning
(Shapiro, p. 55). The combination of the trivialization of labor and
the separation of struggle for meaning into the private realm has
played havoc with any attempt to achieve an education for human
liberation. Without an understanding of genuine self-awareness or
critical consciousness, the assertion of human liberation is turned
back on itself as a means of further repression and accommoda-
tion (Shapiro, p. 100). The body/subject succumbs physically and
emotionally under the ideological force of capitalism.

In this social division, between the domain of being in the
private/home and public/work space, Turner notes, there is also a
sexual division. Divided sexually, the public/producer body is
"asceticised" in contrast to the desires of the private/consumer
body. Situating the female/private body in contradiction to the
male/public body sets up a struggle over the nature of desire.
Turner suggests that under the public/production realm, bodily
desires can become trapped by the dominant consciousness. He
states, "Knowledge produced desire in order to control it" (p. 48).
Bringing together McLaren's modes of production and modes of
desire with Turner's division of male reason and female passion,
I will sketch out what this might mean in conjunction with the
objectification of the female body. The public/producer culture
dominates the socioeconomic reproduction of desires through the
images of those desires as commodified bodies and other objects.
Luce Irigaray (1981) writes, "The trade that organizes patriarchal
societies takes place exclusively among men. Women, signs,
goods, currency, all pass from one man to another (p. 107).

Frigga Haug analyzed the importance attached to the female body in the production of ideological subjugation: "The woman as woman owes her body to a man; as a female human being, she owes him her character. A man, as man, looks to her body; as human being, to her character" (1987, p. 107). The woman's body is positioned in a way that becomes the focal point for the construction of identity. Women have come to construct their identities in relationship to socially constructed notions of the "beautiful female body." What results from this is a consumer society where the female-being ingests these oppressive descriptions of her own subjectivity. She becomes coconspirator to her own oppression as she unquestioningly accepts as her being that which has been constituted through the dominant public discourse of male desire. Frigga Haug (1987) refers to this kind of being as being-as-object.

> It has frequently been suggested that advertising and fashion influence women in what they wear. In this way, it is said, desires are manipulated; or rather, the perpetual creation of new needs leads women to concern themselves with their bodies, their appearance. As far as the activities of the textile industry are concerned, this assumption is clearly to some extent justified. It does not, however, explain why women actually yield to these industries' whispered promises. What causes consumers to purchase any given product is not real use value, but the aesthetics of the commodity as it impinges upon the sensuality of the purchaser. Advertising is only the promise of use value. Desires, hopes and longings are projected upon the surface of the commodity. (pp. 134-135)

One such desire of women is to be desired by men. The desired image, as such, is projected in the social and economic imagery of television, magazines, billboards, books; and more so, by the activities of buying, wearing, exercising, and the fashions of women that form and repress their bodies.

Such critique warrants a radical investigation of dominant consciousness, wherein lies the creation and maintenance of a specific form of human existence. Marcuse (1969) argues that the body most sharply experiences the pain of domination and repression of authentic human desire knowing this in relationship to its memory of happiness and self-fulfillment. Understanding of the forming of subjectivity requires us to go beyond epistemological concerns, and to address issues of power, ideology, and economics. Theoretical discussions must embrace oppressive and resistive elements expressed through, and demonstrated in, the human body.

Human beings form their identities with and through the somatic messages transmitted by the culture in which they live. Without a concrete language of the body we can become lost in a theorizing that is dominated by a masculine discourse and sanctioned within the "objective" language of the technology. To call for a concrete language of the body in the Heideggerian sense, where being, truth, and existence are a single event, points to the impossibility of designating any one particular discourse or single logic for understanding multiple experiences or realities. Behind any attempt to do so lie issues of dogma, reification, and power. We exist within heterogeneous structures. Recalling the body as a locator of the truth of existence—or the reality we live—brings together both reason and sensuality, intellect and perception, mind and body. The struggle to dwell in a discourse of our bodily existence opens us to the struggle to give words to experiential knowledge. Expressed in this is a discourse of subjugated knowledge.

"Subjugated knowledges" is a term used by Foucault to identify a whole group of knowledges that have been either disregarded in an all-encompassing theoretical framework, or erased in a triumphal history of ideas (Sharon Welch, 1985). These knowledges lie beneath the cognitive, scientific-rational ordering of empirical knowledge. One example of such knowledge is that which pertains to the body. Nowhere is this so clear as in the subjugation of women's bodies in the dominant masculine discourse.

Personal knowledge, body politics, and hierarchical-patriarchal discourses are all central issues to the feminist movement. Foucault's work has made apparent what women knowingly live: power is always present in the body because it is coterminous with the conditions of social relations. All relations are social relations, and therefore, contain issues of power.

Foucault (1977, pp. 219-220) states; "The real strength in the women's liberation movement is not that of having laid claim to the specificity of their sexuality and the rights pertaining to it, but that they have actually departed from the discourse conducted within the apparatuses of sexuality." Difficulty arises in creating words to express a foregone text. New "truths" must begin to pass the lips of the oppressed. With the spoken known of body experiences comes the explosion of the old, abstract discourse. Death of the old discourse must occur before there can be new beginnings. Helen Cixous (1981) writes.

> A feminine text cannot fail to be more than subversive. It is volcanic; as it is written it brings about an upheaval of the old property crust, carrier of masculine investments; there's no other way. There's no room left if she's not a he. If she's a her-she, it's in order to smash everything, to shatter the framework of institutions, to blow up the law, to break up the "truth" with laughter. (p. 316)

Discourse, power, and knowledge are inseparable. Throwing off the "old property crust" means first addressing the oppressed nature of a banished knowledge marked on, through, and within the body.

References

Adorno, T., & Horkheimer, M. (1972). *Dialectic of enlightenment* (J. Cumming, Trans.). New York: Herder & Herder.

Berger, J. (1984). *And our faces, my heart, brief as photos.* New York: Pantheon Books.

Berger, J., & Mohr, J. (1982). *Another way of telling.* New York: Pantheon Books.

Bordo, S. (1990). Feminism, postmodernism, and gender-scepticism. In L. J. Nicholson (Ed.), *Feminism/Postmodernism* (pp. 133-157). New York: Routledge.

Brenkman, J. (1987). *Culture and domination.* Ithaca: Cornell University Press.

Cixous, H. (1981). The laugh of the medusa. In E. Marks, & I. de Courtivron (Eds.), *New French feminisms* (pp. 245-263). New York: Schocken Books.

Dworkin, A. (1987). *Intercourse*. London: Arrow Books.

Fay, B. (1987). *Critical social science*. New York: Cornell University.

Foucault, Ml. (1977). *Discipline and punish.* (A. Sheridan, Trans.). New York: Pantheon Books.

Haug, F. (1987). *Female sexualization*. London: Verso.

Heidegger, M. (1968). *What is called thinking.* (F. Wieck, & J. Gray, Trans.). New York: Harper & Row.

Heidegger, M. (1962). *Being and time* (J. Macquarrier, & E. Robinson, Trans.). New York: Harper & Row.

Irigaray, L. (1981). Demystifications. In E. Marks, & I. de Courtivron (Eds.), *New French feminisms* (pp. 99-110). New York: Schocken Books.

Keleman, S. (1981). *Your body speaks its mind*. Berkeley: Center Press.

Lifton, R. (1990). The genocidal mentality. *Tikkun*, 5(3), 29-32 & 97-98.

Marcuse, H. (1969). *Essays on liberation*. Boston: Beacon Press.

McLaren, P. (1989). *Life in schools*. New York: Longman.

McLaren, P. (1988). Schooling the postmodern body: Critical pedagogy and the politics of enfleshment. *Journal of Education*, 170(3), 53-83.

Seidel, G. (1964). *Martin Heidegger and the pre-socratics*. Lincoln: University of Nebraska Press.

Shapiro, H. S. (1990). *Between capitalism and democracy*. New York: Bergin & Garvey.

Turner, B. (1984). *The body and society*. Oxford: Basil Blackwell.

Weiler, K. (1991). Freire and a feminist pedagogy of difference. *Harvard Educational Review*, 61(4), 449-474.

Weiler, K. (1988). *Women teaching for change*. New York: Bergin & Garvey.

Welch, S. (1985). *Communities of solidarity and resistance*. New York: Orbis Books.

Woodman, M. (1985). *The pregnant virgin*. Toronto: Inner City Books.

CHAPTER THREE

Skinned Alive:
Towards a Postmodern Pedagogy of the Body

The body/subject in the modernist rationalist discourse has suffered the effects of alienation in its abstraction of sensual existence and concrete social experience. Rational thinking has left its mark as it has hidden the knowledge of human experience in the separation of objective and subjective worlds. Peter Solterdijk (1987) asserts that "Enlightenment, which strives for the reification and objectification of knowledge, reduces the world of the physiognomic to silence" (p. 140). Postmodernism, in its criticism of these aspects of modernist or enlightenment thinking, has insisted on the particular over the grand scale, the embodied over the abstract, and the sensual/aesthetic over the distantly rational. As a "step-child" of modernist thinking, and despite its emancipatory intent, critical pedagogy has continued to emphasize a notion of intellectual enlightenment that occurs through a process of critical-contextual reflection upon "everyday" existence. From this essentially rationally-based theory of human liberation there has developed a number of criticisms broadly categorized as postmodern. Among the most important of these is the assertion that it represents part of a patriarchal discourse. Feminist theorists such as Elizabeth Ellsworth, Frances Maher, Rhonda Hammer, Michelle Fine, Kathleen Weiler, and Patti Lather indicate the effects such a discourse have on the development of critical pedagogy. One example is given in Frances Maher's article (1987,) that critiques the liberatory model of pedagogy in its disengagement from the particular, a model that remains disconnected from experiential knowing, and therefore the body/subject. "Liberation models of teaching, and Marxist feminism as well," writes

Maher, "often fail to attend to the role of intimacy, of feelings for particular people in particular situations" (p. 97). Phillip Corrigan (1988) in a distinctly postmodern narrative reflects upon the institution of schooling in its relationship to the body. He insists on the need for educational theory to address the "forgotten body."

> All I am trying to say is that bodies matter in schooling. They/we are the subjects who are taught, disciplined, measured, evaluated, examined, passed (or not), assessed, graded, hurt, harmed, twisted, reworked, applauded, praised, encouraged, enforced, coerced, consensed.... To have around volumes of educational theory (however radical) that never mention bodies, and their differentiation, seems to me now, slightly stupid. In a more extended emphasis, bodies may be what (who) is being schooled because by now—I hope—we cannot so easily separate minds, psyches, emotions from bodies. (p. 153)

Postmodern perspectives that derive from Martin Heidegger's relational forms of knowing and existential "truth"; feminist theories that insist on "embodied knowing"; and the work of those like Foucault who have drawn our attention to the "micro physics of power" have laid the basis for a critical pedagogy that takes the body/subject far more seriously. Indeed, within critical pedagogy itself there is now an emerging discourse of the body. Peter McLaren, Michelle Fine, Phillip Corrigan, and others have written on, and raised issues concerning, the social construction of bodies as they are constituted within discourses of race, class, gender, age, and other forms of oppression (Freund, p. 857). The underlying importance of this "body knowledge" for critical educators is that it makes possible new, more intimate, and grounded forms of liberatory praxis. This chapter is a further contribution to the development of a language of a pedagogy that, centered on the body, makes apparent our lives as they are configured in our flesh.

Our Skin: The First Clue to Identity
The skin is the first clue to our identity. Andrea Dworkin (1988, p. 25) captures the intimate and powerful dialectic that connects skin to society.

> The skin is a line of demarcation, a periphery, the fence, the form, the
> shape, the first clue to identity in a society (for instance, color in a
> racist society), and, in purely physical terms, the formal precondition
> for being human.

Body in all its materiality is socially marked and identified as
black, woman, handicapped, old, lower class, fat—as the language of "other." The first clue to identity is the skin you wear.
Dworkin continues:

> It is a thin veil of matter separating the outside from the inside. It is
> what one sees and what one covers up; it shows and it conceals; it
> hides what is inside.

The skin exposes our nationalities, it is implicated in the forming
of gender, and marks the experiences of the "times" we live. To
critically interpret what can be seen in the body of a Southern mill
worker is to understand something about the life of that individual. The walk is distinct: stiff and unyielding, shoulders falling
forward, back rounded placing the head slightly forward and
causing the weight of the body to create an off-balance effect. The
legs seem to be continually trying to "catch-up" with the forward-
falling movement, attempting to make a stance, and yet being
continually pulled off balance. Between upper and lower body is
the gut—the place of connection between "what one thinks" and
"where one stands." The gut of the body can be emaciated, exposing the fleshlessness as the outward signs of the inward empti-
ness. Eyes focus downward, attempting to locate their "grounding," trying to locate the body/subject. At other times the eyes
project a downward gaze in associating "not seeing" with not
"being seen." And there are darting eyes that depict the fear of
"being caught" in the authoritarian gaze. There are, of course,
other "body portraits" that could be critically described (e.g., the
floor supervisor, plant manager, or front-desk receptionist), each
giving insights to "the place" of our bodies in society.

Represented in these bodies is a way of life made manifest in
the skeletal structure, and in the flesh and skin that cover it. Signs
of oppressive lives are the consequence of an economic system that

is parasitic on the flesh and blood of the workers. This system relies on disempowerment through heteronomous structures in which workers retain an insignificant amount of control over their life energies. Movement is mechanized, regulating bodily needs and life schedules to a pattern that fits the production time clocks. And, minds are restricted to thinking in a discourse of mechanical reproduction and technical efficiency. Don Johnson (1983) writes concerning how one's life work shapes one's body and perceptions.

> A worker on an assembly line or a secretary in an office, performing only one kind of action throughout the day, begin to get a sense of their bodies as machines with a narrow range of movement and little feeling. The reduction of the body's capacities to the specific range required by the habitual work correspondingly diminishes the scope of one's perceptions. (p. 78)

Johnson calls this kind of work the "technology of alienation" (p. 80), a way of applying techniques that disconnect people from their sensual being. The body/subject is controlled in a framework structured to alienate them from their own sense of authority in making choices about how they live their lives. We experience feelings of ourselves in different situations. In some instances we might say, "This feels right," or "I don't feel good about this." Turning our sensory powers to how we feel within concrete social situations, as Dorothy Soelle suggests, brings us back in touch with our own capability to make moral choices about what "feels right or wrong."

Without "sensual authority" we can become muscularly rigid and perceptually dulled. Image a man in uniform: molded to the shape of authority, he stands erect as a symbol of hierarchy and a phallocentric culture; expanded chest and jutting chin denote aggressive power; stomach drawn inward, tightening against any "gut" feeling of morality; legs spread apart taking up the space that he feels is rightfully his; the eyes stare coldly straight ahead, acknowledging the impossibility of being directed into an alternative direction. The total image is one of hardness and coldness framed in a uniform that gives him identity and self-worth.

To feel one's own body as oppressed and as the oppressor would be to live with, and within, the body in full recognition of its social and economic structuring. It would be to make concrete one's own existence, and in so doing disclose the oppressive nature of a system where only a few have the privilege of power. It would be to see "what is" of the skins that we wear. The skin bears the content of our lives. The meeting point between outside and inside, Dworkin writes, is the skin. "The skin is separation, individuality, the basis for corporeal privacy and also the point of contact for everything outside of itself. It is the conductor for all feeling" (1988, p. 25). My skin places me within a specific race, gender, and class. I can be identified as a white, middle-class female by what I buy to put on my body (clothes, jewelry, cosmetics). Dworkin contends that it is the skin that is the existential marking between self and world. "Every time the skin is touched, one feels. All feeling passes through it, outside to inside," writes Dworkin. "The skin is our human mask; it is what one can touch of another person, what one sees, how one is seen.... It is both identity and sex what one is and what one feels in the realm of the sensual, being and passion, where the self meets the world—intercourse being, ultimately, the self in the act of meeting the world" (1988, pp. 25-26).

To know our "skinned-over" bodies is to understand, as Dworkin names it, "intercourse being." It is to recognize our deep insertion into the social order. We are coded in the beginning by the color of our skin, sexuality, and the social class of our families. As I was once told by a friend, "You know you could dress Jane up, but she would still look the same." In this statement is the implicit belief that Jane is betrayed by her body, which has been socially inscribed within a historical text and nonverbal cultural language written before her birth. Covering Jane's body with another image cannot hide her social markings. They are too deep.

> One's skin takes on a social function—even naked, one is not purely naked; social identity becomes a new, tough, impermeable skin; one's nakedness if covered over by layers of social self and emotional paint,

rituals and rules, habits of being that are antithetical to any pure experience of being (Dworkin, p. 23).

One's own body is the meeting point between private and public. Fostered in an ideology of individualism is the belief that one's own body is one's own, though in everyday life the power of the state constantly reasserts its control—especially among women (Haug and Foucault). This works, as we know, in contradictory ways. For example, if I am physically assaulted, the attacker may be brought to legal judgment; or if I am murdered there will be legal inquiry. Yet, if I am raped, I may be accused of provoking this assault by "being a certain way"—more commonly referred to as "asking for it"; or if I become pregnant I may or may not have the choice to bring life into the world; or be allowed to act differently than the acceptable "gender-specific" ways. But, as Foucault argues, constitutions of the body take place through the operations of power that exist (not only in the state, but throughout the society and its institutions). This process is what Frigga Haug (1987) calls "sexualization"—the gendered constitution of the body. Sexualization does not simply refer to the sexuality of the body, rather it encompasses the totality of how one is constructed within sociocultural norms.

Being-Skinned Alive

To work within a particular economic structure is to be inserted into a way of life that appropriates one's productive energies for specific purposes. John Berger powerfully describes the body inscriptions of five Turkish workers:

> Five of the men are workers.... One is bald, one has curly hair, two are thin and wiry, one is broad-shouldered and well-covered. All are wearing skimpy, cheap trousers and jackets. Those clothes bear the same relation to the suits of the bourgeoisie as the capital's shanty-towns, where the five live, bear to the villas with French furniture where the bosses and merchants live. Yet, with their clothes taken off, in a public bath, a police or army officer would have little difficulty in identifying them as workers. Even if the five half-closed their eyes so

as to mask their expressions, so as to pretend to a commendable indifference, their social class would still be evident....

It is as if a court, at the moments of their conception had sentenced them all to have their heads severed from their necks at the age of fifteen. When the time came, they resisted, as all workers resist, and their heads remained on their shoulders. But the tensions and obstinacy of that resistance has remained, and still remains, visible—there between the nape of the neck and the shoulder blades. Most workers in the world carry the same physical stigma: a sign of how the labor power of their bodies has been wrenched away from their heads, where their thoughts and imagining continue, but deprived now of the possession of their own days and working energies.

Berger continues:

For the five in the wood-paneled room, resistance is more than a reflex, more than the muscles' primitive refusal of what the body knows to be an injustice—because what its effort is continually creating is immediately and irredeemably taken out of its hands. Their resistance has mounted, and entered their thoughts, their hopes, their explanations of the world. The five heads, whose eyes pierce me, have declared their bodies, not only resistant, but militant. (1984, pp. 16-17)

The men have claimed the injustice of what their bodies know and termed it intolerable. Naming the intolerable must pre-exist change. In this naming, the existential issues are brought to examination. William Pinar (1981) suggests that when one is psychologically present rather than emotionally numbed, one can attune oneself to a situation, and thus become conscious of how life history, commitments, and assumptions operate in our experience of that situation. Pinar argues that as one becomes conscious of them one can become free of them. The articulation of situations is what focuses or attunes us to our life-world, allowing the problematic to be revealed. Pinar writes that the, "situation comes to form through us, and thus our sensibilities do not merely precondition knowledge; they make it possible" (p. 180).

The capacity to articulate comes with an understanding of the human condition as formed by past experiences, and with a recognition of future possibilities. Memories of life where one is able to touch, be touched, feel and respond, becomes the ever-nagging memory within the human body; the desire for pleasure, and for intimacy as experienced in flesh and blood. Vincent Geoghegan (1988) refers to Marcuse's work when he writes, "Such memory is a spur to change; it is an actual and powerful goad to re-create the lost conditions of happiness, for the past continues to reclaim the future" (p. 102).

The communion is between past, present, and future in a unifying contextual knowledge that breaks down the barriers held in the ever-present now. Berger (1984) writes, "The time of the torturers is agonizingly in the present" (p. 18). What is significant here is the value placed upon critical understanding of history as something that carries with it the past as well as possibilities for the future. Inherent in this kind of understanding is that wo/man is not a passive recipient of this world and can act to change it. This knowledge is a threat to the status quo—to the "torturers of the present."

A Political Collaboration:
Giving up Freedom for Compliance

To look to the future with hope is to desire something different from what is. Yet, to understand the female body in the present culture is to critically apprehend the way oppression is not merely imposed, but an act of participation by those who are oppressed.

Feminists write about being female in the context of power over the female body by men. Dworkin states: "Male power may be arrogant or elegant; it can be churlish or refined; but we exist as persons to the extent that men in power recognize us" (1988, p. 150). This hierarchical organization of power sustains itself in the conceptualization of male activity and female passivity. Helene Cixous (1981) charges that this conceptualization places women always on the side of passivity, and as "other." To be passive is to become a participant in one's own oppression. To be "other" places her in relationship to man as always being "body." Cixous (1981) with other French feminists, argues that, more so than men, women are body. Yet the life energy of the woman as body is directed toward the male image of desire. Feminist writers have made clear the objectification of woman's body in the attempt to remake and reshape it into an ornament of desire. The body as desired object typically has pouting lips, silky long hair, enfleshed breasts, provocative eyes, long legs, shapely "ass," and as object is displayed to draw the male gaze towards the center of her sexual being through explicit exaggeration. Her being becomes the physical representation of male desire. Dworkin elaborates on the male objectification of the female body:

> Being an object—living in the realm of male objectification—is abject submission, an abdication of the freedom and integrity of the body, its privacy, its uniqueness, its worth in and of itself because it is the human body of a human being.... To become an object she takes herself and transforms herself into a thing: all freedoms are diminished and she is caged, even in the cage docile, sometimes physically maimed, movement is limited... (1988, p. 166)

This system of objectification as a strategy of domination is referred to in feminist writing as "colonization." The woman takes on the burden, the responsibility, of her own submission, and her own objectification. By internalizing the ideas of what is valued in women (by the dominant male structure), she constructs herself according to those objectified ideas or images. Collaborating with her own submission implies an acceptance of a system that gives her object status. It is an implicit acceptance of less freedom, less power, less dignity; she becomes something less than equal. Hers is a political collaboration in that the act of collaboration is an acceptance of Hegel's "master-slave" relationship. Dworkin (p. 167) contends that there is an initial complicity in the act of confirming oneself as something rather than someone. In this initial complicity there are the acts of self-mutilation, self-diminishment, and self-deconstruction, until there is no self, no memories. The alienation from worth as a human being is fundamental to female objectification. This alienation is the grounding that undermines the values of human dignity for self and for others. Without knowing one's own human value the possibilities for a sense of human justice or freedom is diminished. "Something happens inside," writes Dworkin, " a human forgets freedom; a human learns obedience; a human, this time a woman, learns how to goose-step the female way" (1988, p. 167). The act goes beyond complicity to collaboration. Collaboration of this sort requires the undermining of values and dignity—an alienation from worth as a human being to one of merely exchange value; and, therefore, an alienation from human freedom that is deep and destructive. Dworkin continues, "it destroys whatever it is in us as humans that is creative, that causes us to want to find meaning in experiences, even hard experiences; it destroys in us that which wants freedom, whatever the hardships of attaining it" (p. 168).

The objectification and oppression of women finds its parallel in the life of all human beings described as "other"—for foreign-born workers, Jews, blacks, gays, physically and mentally differently abled—any human being who is dehumanized for the sake of another. Compliance to, and collaboration with, such efforts strips away human capacities to imagine a different relationship to others and to our world. As Haug has noted, women in contemporary society mourn our lack of desire for a different relationship with the world. Her statement speaks to women who struggle with the hegemonic relationship between themselves and the world. What is to be understood is that we can never be outside of our own social construction or the dominant consciousness that is embedded in our very subjectivity. Women, in capitalist culture, are limited, restricted, and reduced as their bodies and senses are appropriated by either economic or sexual language. As such, the attention of women is turned toward their bodies (i.e., women are constantly bombarded with advertising directed toward "make-overs"—if only you buy this product, or do this to your skin, or change your hair color or style, you too can be more beautiful, more sexy, or more likely to get the job or raise you want; overall the message is "if you buy this, you can become this). Women are made to constantly confront their own imperfect bodies. Something is to be hidden (cottage-cheese thighs), shaped (buns of steel), toned-up (flabby tummy), or criticized (being too short). The boundaries of this ordering of existence reek with oppression and subordination, and are shot through with questions about the delineated boundaries of human identity. Internalizing the "norms" or standards of being a beautiful woman, and therefore a valuable human being, does more than produce desired images. There is also an acceptance of a particular identity and a particular relationship to others. One can become businesslike, sexy, motherly, punk, conservative, athletic, girlish, sophisticated, intellectual, liberal, or "loose," all informed by these socially-constructed images. What is revealed are the heteronomous structures that enclose the body (Haug, 1987). Character is assimilated into social images; the resulting character appears "real"—the "natural" you.

The Corporeality of Language

Feminist writers suggest "writing the body." This means including the knowledge of the body in the language of the mind. "Isn't the final goal of writing to articulate the body? For me the sensual juxtaposition of words has one function: to liberate a living paste, to liberate matter" (Albright, 1989: p. 35). Chantal Chawaf (1981), with other French feminists, struggled against varied forms of exploitation and against forms of domination through a process that focuses upon putting the feeling, breathing, living bodies of women back into language. Chawaf writes, "Linguistic flesh has been puritanically repressed. Abstraction has starved the language, but words must die. They have a censorial quality. Their role is to develop consciousness and knowledge by liberating our unconscious as well as bringing back hope" (p. 177). She calls for women to reject "fleshless" language in order to emerge from oppression. The feminist language must materialize through the rediscovered body. Another French feminist, Luce Irigaray, cautions about the return to the body when she writes, "Female sexuality has always been theorized within masculine parameters.... Women's desire most likely does not speak the same language as man's desire, and it probably has been covered over by a logic that has dominated the West since the Greeks" (1981, p. 99). To problematize the masculine discourse, and its possession over the female body, through a sexualization process that objectifies it under the "prevalence of the gaze," returns us to the relationship between ways of thinking and ways of being. Simply stated, the question that concerns us is the way individual lives are dominated by the prevalent form of knowing; that is, the form which has structured "seeing" as knowing. Irigaray contends that this masculine logic is in opposition to a feminine relational way of knowing; a way of knowing that is embodied as touch (1981, p.101). Yet, the mode of exchange that organizes a standard for human pleasure and desire is regulated by the masculine mode of desire. As postmodern thinkers such as Foucault and Lyotard have asserted, this mode focuses upon objectified images consti-tuted through "sight" rather than touch. For women, questions arise, such as: "How can a female-object begin to liberate her own human desires without an immense upheaval of the estab-lished market and merchandising economic system in, by, and for men?" and "How can the move be made from abstract seeing to concrete touching?"

Marguerite Duras (1981) strikes out at the slow-dying mas-culine-based knowledge system:

> Men are regressing everywhere, in all areas.... The capacity on which men judge intelligence is still the capacity to theorize. It has been under attack for centuries. It ought to be crushed by now, it should lose itself in a reawakening to the senses, blind itself, and be still. (p. 111)

Duras's anger is directed toward the continuing use of the "old ways of theorizing" to recount and relate to new situations. For it these "old" paradigms that distance and objectify, in which other forms of knowing are suffocated. French feminism, in general, has represented a movement that protests the indignities project-ed onto the image of the female body, and that pleads for women to speak out from their oppressed position by rewriting, respeak-ing, and repositioning themselves in a history yet to be heard. They recognize the necessity and possibility for human beings to be jolted out of embeddedness, to be interrupted from routinized behaviors, and to respond with the desires that inform us of our human need for touch, relationship, and love. The female body can only be released from its masculine ownership through awareness by both men and women.

To connect these issues to the larger problems of humanity makes them political issues and reduces the possibility that they become co-opted by society as specifically women's problems. Arlette Laguiller (1981) writes:

> Feminism, except on very limited issues (abortion) cannot bring together all women in common struggle. Class oppression is stronger.... I have never known women who had emancipated themselves on the woman question before they had emancipated themselves on the political question. (p. 123)

Human beings produce their lives collectively. The issue of the "objectified body" as an oppressive social element is not only an issue for women, but also of the working class as a whole. To address feminist issues is to address issues of the collective social production where modes of subjective appropriation can be generalized. Christine Delphy (1981), in recognizing the relationship of individual experience to the larger social relations, states that feminism is first of all a social movement of liberation. Oppression has to be the starting point for the explanation of human history. This then becomes a materialist liberation where explanations cannot be limited to any one oppression, or leave untouched any part of reality, any domain of knowledge, any aspect of the world. Delphy argues that "feminism-as-a-movement aims at the revolution of social reality, so feminism-as-a-theory must aim at the revolution of knowledge" (p. 198). Liberation as the basis for critical pedagogy then must involve, as feminists argue, a rejection of the prevalent masculine way of knowing, to one which is relationally understood, and grounded in the experiential and intuitive knowledge held in our bodies. To understand personal experiences is to remember and reflect upon these memories in all their social relatedness. Yet, we have come to privatize our memories, isolating resistant actions from the public realm. Without the capacity to critically link the individual to the life-world in terms of social relationships, resistance in any form is limited to an overly personalized one. As suggested by Peter Solterdijk, this produces the contradictions felt in modern consciousness wherein the separation of the rational (what we claim as truth), and the real (what we experientially know as truth) grow further apart.

The Body in Resistance: We Shall Not Be Moved

To understand the lack of social resistance, John Berger (1982) has directed our attention to the way in which time and history become conflated, and therefore personal experiences are invalidated. Personal histories that are either assimilated to the "great narratives of human history," or totally silenced (as black history, women's history, and the history of those "others" whose stories would contradict the "official story"), leaving no trace of the concreteness of existence (Welch, 1985). The destruction and suffering of the oppressed is a story left untold. The history told is that of the dominating class. Yet, Berger notes, this history is far from being totally accepted. There remains an opposition to the violence done to our subjective experiences; to the superseding of particular personal stories by the "official" one of the "grand" narrative. The impossibility to make one's life experiences "fit" into the discourse of another's history provides the impetus for resistance. Berger (1982) writes:

> Revolutionary actions are rare. Feelings of opposition to history, however, are constant, even if inarticulated. They often find their expression in what is called private life.... People's opposition to history is a reaction against violence done to them. The violence consists in conflating time and history so that the two become indivisible, so that people can no longer read their experience of either of them separately. (p. 105)

Berger (1982) suggests that, unfortunately, personal memories are restricted to private thoughts and personal conversations, not to be found in the grand histories of wars, declarations, and discoveries. The everyday occurrences of human experience are eliminated with the sweeping motion of an exclusivist historical discourse. Humans become subjected to objectified history; a history calculated to meet the special demands of telling the "correct stories"—those that prove the accomplishments and therefore the wisdom of the dominant ideology.

Yet elements of resistance are held within our bodies—feelings of defiance that tell another kind of history. Maya Angelou (1990) movingly captures these moments of resistance held in the memories of the black woman's body in her poem "Our Grandmothers." I quote from the poem:

> She lay, skin down on the moist dirt,
> the canebrake rustling
> with the whispers of leaves, and
> loud longing of hounds and
> the ransack of hunters crackling the near branches.
> She muttered, lifting her head a nod towards freedom,
> I shall not, I shall not be moved.
> She gathered her babies,
> their tears slick as oil on black faces,
> their young eyes canvassing mornings of madness.
> Momma, is Master going to sell you
> from us tomorrow?
> Yes.
> Unless you keep walking more
> and talking less.
> Yes.
> Unless the keeper of our lives
> releases me from all commandments.
> Yes.
> And your lives,
> never mine to live
> will be executed upon the killing floor of the innocents.
> Unless you match my heart and words,
> saying with me,
> I shall not be moved.
>
> Her universe, often
> summarized into one black body
> falling finally from the tree to her feet,
> made her cry each time in a new voice.
> All my past hastens to defeat,

and strangers claim the glory of my love,
Iniquity has bound me to this bed,
yet, I must not be moved.

She heard the names,
swirling ribbons in the wind of history:
nigger, bitch, heifer,
mammy, property, creature, ape, baboon.
whore, hot tail, thing, it.
She said, But my description cannot
fit your tongue, for
I have a certain way of being in this world,
and I shall not, I shall not be moved.

These momma faces, lemon-yellow, plum-purple,
honey-brown, have grimaced and twisted
down a pyramid of years.
She is Sheba and Sojourner,
Harriet and Zora,
Mary Bethune and Angela,
Annie to Zeobia.
She stands
before the abortion clinic,
confounded by the lack of choices.
In the Welfare line,
reduced to the pity of handouts.
Ordained in the pulpit, shielded
by the mysteries.
In the operating room,
husbanding life.
In the choir loft,
holding God in her throat
On lonely street corners,
hawking her body.
In the classroom, loving the
children to understanding.
Centered on the world's stage,
she sings to her loves and beloveds,
to her foes and detractors:
However I am perceived and deceived,
however my ignorance and conceits,
lay aside your fears that I will be undone,
for I shall not be moved.

However powerful the memories of actual human experiences are, without the sharing of these stories, instances of resistance are lost, and with them possibility for liberation. Sharon Welch refers to Mary Daly's work in the description of the interaction between personal and political liberation. Welch (1985) writes:

> As women share stories of their own lives, a common experience of oppression and resistance is recognized. This politicization gives women the courage to persist in resistance, recognizing their difficulties have not only individual basis but social and political bases as well. (p. 41)

Without the communal sharing of life stories, concerns, and griefs, the solidarity that Welch writes about cannot develop, and social change can be misdirected and limited.

Cynical Reason and Kynical Resistance
Peter Solterdijk (1987), the influential German scholar, theorizes the preeminence of privatized resistance in bodily forms. In modern society he poses a description of the body that responds to the cynicism of domination with satirical laughter, defiant body actions, or strategic silence. He calls this bodily response "kynical resistance." In creating this "situated body response" to the cynical consciousness of the modern human condition, he restates the impossibility of self-language without worldly language. In the notion of kynicism as a bodily physical response to the "situation" of one's life (even though unconscious), lies the bodily dissonance between "how one lives," and "how one feels about the life condition."

Cynicism as repression is, for Solterdijk, the other side of kynicism. Indeed, he perceives cynicism as the predominant mind set of the post-1960's era.

> It articulates an uneasiness that sees the modern world steeped in cultural insanities, false hopes and their disappointment, in the progress of madness and the suspension of reason, in the deep schism that runs through modern consciousness and that seems to separate the rational

and the real, what we know and what we do, from each other for all time. (p. 217)

Cynical thinking can only become possible when two different views of the world are seen in their contradictory relationship; namely an official view and an unofficial view. This concept of cynicism produces a corresponding though opposite form of expression, kynicism. Kynicism is, as explained by Solterdijk,

> the urge of individuals to maintain themselves as fully rational living beings against the distortions and semi-rationalities of their societies. Existence in resistance, in laughter, in refusal, in the appeal of the whole of nature and a full life. It begins as plebeian "individualism," pantomimic, wily, and quick witted. (pp. 217-218)

Kynical impulses are widely displayed in the "clash of consciousness" as they are written on and acted out with our bodies. Following are examples Solterdijk provides in his chapter, "Concerning the Psychosomatics of the Zeitgeist":

> When we quarrel passionately, we often come to the point where words are not enough. The body knows how to help: We stick out our tongues and make a noise that makes it clear what we think of the other person....
>
> A crooked smile, an evilly clever gesture, easily arises out of crooked superiority. One corner of the mouth, often the left corner, is drawn upward. On the mouth of the master, the split of consciousness becomes visible; the other half knows there is really nothing to laugh about.... The worldly realism of the master cynic comes from the wise to save face while he is getting his hands dirty....

The life experience of victims are revealed in their bitterness. On their lips a bitter silence forms....

> The cynical gaze lets things know that they do not exist as real objects for it, but only as a phenomena and information. It looks at them as if they already belong to the past. In modern civilization of media and fashion, an atmospheric concoction of cosmetics, pornography, consumerism, illusion, addiction, and prostitution reigns for which the baring and depiction of breasts is typical. In the commodity world, it

seems that nothing functions without them any more... Sexism? If it were only that simple.... These modern business breasts exist, philosophically speaking, only in themselves, as things, not for themselves, as conscious bodies.

The arse doomed to spend its life in the dark, as the beggar among body parts.... The arse is the plebeian, the grass-roots democrat, and the cosmopolitan among the parts of the body—in a word, the elementary kynical organ. It provides the solid materialist basis. It is at home on all toilets all over the world.

The attempt of Solterdijk is to integrate philosophy (and its concerns with the "great problems," of our world) with the concerns of the "trivial everyday life." The world situation, he argues, can be found in our bones, our nerves, our eyes, and even in the corners of our mouths. Indeed, the possibility for what he calls kynical responses to the cynicism of the modern world is crucial. Here is where our humanity resides and pokes out at the world in response to the conditions we find ourselves in. Solterdijk (1987) identifies a subjectivity that "in spite of the horror of socialization" rejects distancing and objectification for "physiognomic thought which poses a sense of warmth and intimacy, convivial knowledge, and a libidinous closeness to the world that compensates for the objectifying drive toward the domination of things" (p. 140). The hope is for the synchronization of self and worldly experience; a consciousness that can enfold our privatized and individualized selves into the greater "whole" of human experience.

His approach shares common ground with critiques of Western rationality and patriarchy as they have been articulated in the postmodern discourses of ecology, Lacanian psychoanalysis, feminism, and radical theology. These discourses offer a critique of the regime of disembodied thought and they articulate a language of flesh-and-blood realities. Their attempt is to announce a new critique of reason that asserts the inseparability of mind and body, thought and life.

Examples of kynical resistance can also be found in studies of popular culture. Leslie Roman, in one such study, examined the cultural production of femininity in the ritual of creating the punk "slam dance." Her study gives examples of kynical resistance. The following is a description of one young woman's euphoric experience sustained when dancing.

> When I get out there on the dance-floor I close my eyes. I almost never have my eyes open when dancing.... This is going to sound really sappy or something, but you saw *Star Wars*, right? You know that "Force"—that thing that went through the whole movie? Well, I feel like that when I'm dancing.... I feel like I'm really going into something. I get this sensation of being part of this huge, like, a whirlpool or something, and letting myself go into it. I'm not aware of my body; it's just another thing for me personally... In a way I feel separated from my body in the fact that it's there doing something that I don't normally do in an interaction with other people with my body. It's nice. I'm not aware of pain a whole lot when I get my adrenaline going, which is scary. And that happens to me in basketball or soccer. You know, I'll sprain my ankle...which is dangerous not feeling it, but I like feelings of just being so active it hurts. It's like the kind of pain that's satisfying. I don't mean that to sound sadistic or masochistic— I always get those two mixed up. It's just that some things are really satisfying as much as it may hurt me or wear me down. I feel like I've accomplished something just getting women out there on the dance floor. (1988, p. 160)

Dancing becomes an extraordinary moment of transcendence. In this state of euphoria there is a relationship between the pleasure of such a mode of disembodiment (transcending the body), and the desire to celebrate actively the whole feminine body rather than "give status to certain parts of the body as sexual fetishes for male eroticism" (Roman, Christian-Smith, & Ellsworth, 1988: p. 160). Dancing, in this sense, challenges the idea of feminine bodily fragmentation and objectification. However, this kind of kynical resistance is both temporary and partial. For, as already argued, any resistance without "critical grounding" is limited in its effects on our everyday existence.

There are, of course, other images we can call upon to provide examples of the body as the material expression of resistance, and the struggle for political and social liberation. Imagine, for example, South Africans rhythmically moving, filling the space between what they know as slavery and what they aspire to as freedom. They pulsate with an energy that is filled with life, pounding out with every step the defiant anger that sounds the demand for some control over their own lives. Moving together, right arm raised, fist clenched, up and down, yet not touching. They present an image of solidarity. Their bodies speak the words of resistance; they dance on the ground of freedom. They sweat, smelling of the struggle for life. Behind the images their bodies make is the defiance of a political and economic system that names them as Black, and therefore, less than those who are White and control their world.

Less obvious forms of resistance are found throughout society. The work of the German theorist Frigga Haug and her colleagues provides an example of research that, in the interest of human liberation, focuses on contextualizing women's relationship to their own bodies. The formation of sexuality and individuation contain moments of both their submission and resistance to dominant notions of what it is to be a woman. Their research focuses upon the everyday taken-for-grantedness of women's existence, and takes the form of critical reflection upon the narratives of their own lives. These stories are retold from childhood memories that were centered around issues of the body. Among these were ones that revealed attempts by parents to instill in their daughters the correct ways of being a "nice" or "good" girl. One such reflection pertained to legs. Commands such as "keep your legs together while sitting" (knees touching, both feet on the floor, and ankles crossed) hold the secret to becoming a respectable woman. Many young women struggle through hours of trying to keep their legs together, keeping their virtue enclosed—whether sitting on gym bleachers or church pews. Yet look at young women today. Positions of sitting cross-legged, one foot on the floor while the other is perched on the chair or some other place denies the conventionality of the "togetherness of the legs," and defies virtue as connected to the "correct" behavior of the person to be displayed by the body form.

Our bodies speak to the growing awareness of the structuring of subjectivity through the "embodiment" of the dominant ideology. Yet, to move beyond unconscious challenges or emotional defiance, there has to be a critical connection able to thread together the fragments of the contradictions, accommodations, and resistances. This is the task of a critical pedagogy, which addresses itself to the question of the body in both the institutional order and in the popular culture.

References

Albright, A. C. (1989). Writing the moving body: Nancy Stark Smith and the hieroglyphs. *Frontiers*, X (3),35.

Angelou, M. (1990). *I shall not be moved*. New York: Random House.

Berger, J., & Mohr, J. (1982). *Another way of telling*. New York: Pantheon Books.

Berger, J. (1984). *And our faces, my heart, brief as photos*. New York: Pantheon Books.

Cixous, H. (1981). The laugh of the medusa. In E. Marks, & I. de Courtivron (Eds.), *New French feminisms* (pp. 245-263). New York: Schocken Books.

Corrigan, P. (1988). The making of the body: Meditations on what grammar school did, with, to, and for my body. *Journal of Education*, *3*, 142-161.

Duras, M. (1981). Warnings. In E. Marks, & I. de Courtivron (Eds.), *New French feminisms* (pp. 111-113). New York: Schocken Books.

Dworkin, A. (1988). *Intercourse*. London: Arrow Books.

Ellsworth, E. (1989). Why doesn't this feel empowering? Working through the repressive myths of critical pedagogy. *Harvard Educational Review*, 59(3), 297-324.

Fine, M. (1991). *Framing dropouts: Notes on the politics of an urban public high school*. Albany: State University Press of New York Press.

Foucault, M. (1980). In C. Gordon (Ed.), *Power/knowledge: Selected interviews and other writings*. Sydney, Australia: Feral Publications.

Freund, P. (1988). Bringing society into the body. *Theory & Society*, 17, 839-864.

Geoghegan, V. (1987). *Utopianism and marxism.* London: Methuen.

Hammer, R. & McLaren, P. ((1989). Critical pedagogy and the postmodern challenge. *Educational Foundations.* 3(3), 29-62.

Haug, F. (1987). *Female sexualization: A collective work of memory.* (E. Carter, trans.). London: Verso

Irigaray, L. (1981). Demystifications. In E. Marks, & I. de Courtivron (Eds.), *New french feminisms* (pp. 99-110). New York: Schocken Books.

Johnson, D. (1983). *Body.* Boston: Beacon Press

Laguiller, A. (1981). Warnings. In E. Marks, & I. de Courtivron (Eds.), *New French feminisms* (pp. 121-124). New York: Schocken Books.

Lather, P. (1991). *Getting smart: Feminist research and pedagogy with/in the postmodern.* New York: Routledge.

Maher, F. A. (1987). Toward a richer theory of feminist pedagogy: A comparison of "liberation" and "gender" models for teaching & learning. *Journal of Education, 169,* (3), 91-100.

Marks, E., & de Courtivron, I. (Eds.) (1981). New French feminisms. New York: Shocken Books.

McLaren. P. (1991). Schooling of the postmodern body: Critical pedagogy and the politics of enfleshment. In H.A. Giroux (Ed.), *Postmodernism, feminism, and cultural politics* (pp. 144- 173). Albany: State University of New York Press.

Pinar, W. (1981). Whole, bright, deep with understanding: Issues of qualitative research and autobiographical method. *Curriculum Studies, 13,* (3), 173-188.

Roman, L.G., Christian-Smith, L. K., & Ellsworth, E. (Eds.) (1988). *Becoming feminine.* London: The Falmer Press.

Soelle, D., & Cloyes, S.A. (1984). *To work and to love: A theology of creation.* Philadelphia: Fortress Press.

Solterdijk, P. (1987). *Critique of cynical reason.* Minneapolis: University of Minnesota Press.

Welch, S. (1985). *Communities of resistance and solidarity.* New York: Orbis Books.

CHAPTER FOUR

Re-Membering the Body in Critical Pedagogy

The Body in Postmodern/Feminist Thought

As we have seen in the previous chapter, postmodern and feminist theorists have recently explored the "situated" (or perhaps more appropriately stated, the "unsituated") body. The disembodied discourse of epistemological objectivity and neutral judgement has been referred to as "the view from nowhere." It has prompted such questions as: Whose Truth? Whose nature? Whose version of reason? Whose history? Whose tradition? (Bordo, 1990). These critiques of abstract theorizing stand against the ideal of disembodied knowledge and hold out significant possibilities for extending the meaning and value of feminist and critically-oriented pedagogy.

There is, we have come to recognize, no Archimedean viewpoint; rather, knowledge is always situated and constructed in a dialectical relationship between the individual and the culture in which she or he lives. For this reason, a great deal of feminist work has attempted to ground knowledge in the body. The body comes to be seen as the preeminent material upon which inscriptions of culture and its particular discourses become embedded. These inscriptions regulate the ways we think and live our social relations. They are constructed in multiple ways (i.e., race, class, gender, age, physical size). What is emphasized here is that *there is no view from nowhere*—no subject situated outside of an historical and cultural context. It contradicts the dualist legacy of Cartesian epistemology in which the goal is to transcend the distortions of feelings and body. To achieve this "God's-eye view," one must "see" objectively, undistorted by human experience and emotions. Yet, in feminist and postmodern discourses the body's place is reconceived. It becomes impossible to transcend. The latter is reconceptualized as the material presence that relativizes perception and thought as it fixes the knower in time and space. In his book, *The Ideology of the Aesthetic,* the influential scholar Terry Eagleton takes up and elaborates the philosophical themes that have emerged in recent feminist and postmodern theorizing. I have found his work to be especially supportive of my own thinking in the connections he draws between the colonization of reason and the subjugation of the body's experiences. He states, "A recovery of the importance of the body has been one of the most precious achievements of recent radical thought" (1990, p. 7). For Eagleton the discourse of the body is synonymous with the aesthetic. The aesthetic refers to the whole region of human perception and sensation—the body experiencing. Eagleton gives insight to the philosophical exclusions and the deeper political and cultural hegemony from which it is born.

> The distinction which the term 'aesthetic' initially enforces in the mid-eighteenth century is not one between 'art' and 'life,' but between material and immaterial: between things and thoughts, sensations and ideas, that which is bound up with your creaturely life as opposed to that which conducts some shadowy existence in the recesses of the mind. It is as though philosophy suddenly wakes up to the fact that there is a dense, swarming territory beyond its own mental enclave which threatens to fall utterly outside its sway. That territory is nothing less than the whole of sensate life together—the business of affections and aversions, of how the world strikes the body on its sensory surfaces, of that which takes root in the gaze and the guts and all that arises from our most banal, biological insertion into the world. *The aesthetic concerns this most gross and palpable dimension of the human, which post-Cartesian philosophy, in some curious lapse of attention, has somehow managed to overlook. It is thus the first stirrings of a primitive materialism—of the body's long inarticulate rebellion against the tyranny of the theoretical* [emphasis added]. (p. 13)

In his history of Western thought, the concern with the "absolute monarch of Reason" has become alienated from philosophy as the breathing, sentient life. The quest, here, is not to surrender to the "subjective," but rather to bring the subjective into the scope of reason, and further acknowledge that reasoning itself does not occur somewhere outside the particular hermeneutic derived from one's experiences; reason itself is inseparable from the language, experience, and culture of historically and socially situated human beings.

This notion of situated knowledge as it is incorporated by the human subject, and as it is inscribed in and on the body as a lived process, is the central focus of this chapter. In particular, the attempt is to demonstrate how the body becomes a vehicle for oppression, as well as resistance, and liberation. I describe the body/subject as one that can be hegemonically inscribed in a particular culture, while at the same time consciously engaged in resisting and/or changing the culture. The shift in my work is from one of detached, abstract discourses of knowledge, thinking about thinking, to a situated concern for human freedom. It speaks to a process of bringing to awareness, through critical reflection, the sociohistorical and cultural inscriptions that, through one's body, shape a life, and through this knowledge make possible the questioning and re-creation of the human condition.

Perception, interpretation, and articulation reveals to us the knowledge of life as "the out-pressing of what we have taken in and contained" (Keleman, p. 130). "Taking in" and "containing" suggest the bodily holding of both oppressive and resistant knowledge. Toni Morrison in her novel *Beloved* exquisitely captures this body knowledge in the following description.

Here [said Baby Suggs] in this here place, we flesh; flesh that weeps, laughs; flesh that dances on bare feet in grass. Love it. Love it hard. Yonder they do not love your flesh. They despise it. They don't love your eyes; they'd just as soon pick em out. No more do they love the skin on your back. Yonder they flay it! And O my people they do not love your hands. Those they only use, tie, bind, chop off and leave empty. Love your hands! Love them.... And no, they ain't in love with your mouth. Yonder, out there, they will see it broken and break it again. What you say out of it they will not heed. What you scream from it they do not hear. What you put into it to nourish your body they will snatch away and give you leavins instead. No they don't love your mouth. *You* got to love it. This is flesh I'm talking about here. Flesh that needs to be loved. Feet that need to rest and to dance;

backs that need support; shoulders that need arms, strong arms I'm
telling you. And O my people, out yonder, hear me, they do not love
your neck unnoosed and straight. So love you neck; put a hand on it,
grace it, stroke it and hold it up. And all your inside parts that they'd
just as soon slop for hogs, you got to love them. The dark, dark
liver—love it, love it, and the beat and beating heart, love that too.
More than eyes or feet. More than lungs that have yet to draw free air.
More than your life-holding womb and your life-giving private parts,
hear me now, love your heart. For this is the prize. (1987, p. 88-9)

Morrison captures the struggle of the oppressed to free themselves as collaborators of their own oppression, to reform their
being through acceptance and love, to redefine the racists' gaze,
to reclaim the body as subject. We can understand Morrison's literary description through Peter McLaren's (1989) theoretical
term of "cultural tattooing"—a process in which elements of the
dominant ideology are "pressed" into the flesh, elements that can
be resisted and subverted through a narrative of bodily affirmation and corporeal reappropriation. It is this task that an embodied critical pedagogy must choreograph in the intimate act of
teaching.

Towards an Embodied Voice in Critical Pedagogy

Clearly the work cited here and in the previous chapter—in the
ways we perceive, live in, live with, and through our bodies—
provide a rich source for gaining understanding the complex and
often contradictory ways in which the subject is positioned in
society, and further provide "body memories," which can reveal
through critical reflection the relationship between ourselves,
others and the world in which we live.

While a number of those concerned with the development of
critical pedagogy (see for example the work of Henry Giroux,
Peter McLaren, Kathleen Weiler, Rhonda Hammer, Phillip
Corrigan, or Michelle Fine) have given attention to the absence of
body knowledge in this pedagogy, there are still few examples
that really illustrate what this might mean. Indeed, some of what
has been written is at such a high level of abstraction that it provides a language far removed from the purported concreteness of

embodied lives. My own work on the body has developed out of my experiences as a dancer, choreographer, woman, and teacher. Paradoxically, my thirty-year involvement in dance can be described as the opposite extreme of disembodiment. Indeed to be in dance subsequently means to be "all body" with no reflection or connection to any kind of theory other than a description of dance genre and technique. The body/subject in dance is defined and refined as body/object or instrument. Here, "disembodiment" refers to a decontextualization of the subject from his or her life experiences or social context. The redefining of "body knowledge" from a technical discourse to a critical one has become the discursive and pedagogic field in which I struggle. The significance of the body in both feminist and critical pedagogies provided the base from which my research, writing, and practice became directed, exploring what a critical pedagogy of the body might mean in dance education as well as in education in general.

I start from the assumption that critical pedagogy is a philosophy of praxis concerned with emancipation, and committed to a process that connects self-reflection and understanding to a knowledge that makes transformation of the social conditions we live possible (Shapiro, 1991). It begins by making it possible for the silenced voices of students to speak in the classroom about their own experiences, concerns, and desires. It therefore remakes the curriculum into a dialectic between their particular hermeneutic of the lived world and the explanatory narrative of a critical theoretical framework. Without either the personal narrative or the critical framework, the pedagogy is incomplete. Without the personal narrative, one cannot articulate or begin to problematize one's everyday existence needed for conscious decision making. And without a critical framework, the personal narrative is privatized, hindering relational understanding of the social forces which structure existence.

The purpose of the following section is to exemplify a critical pedagogy that includes the body as a site for critical reflection and understanding of one's life-world. The body, (and here, my body), has been conceived of in this work as the interface of the individual and society; as the "terrain of flesh" where ideological structures are inscribed; as the material base that holds knowledge; and as that which can "tell the stories" of the lives we live. I have attempted to illustrate how, through the re-collection of my own body memories, the body marks a crucial juncture where we can begin to make sense of the connections between the individual and the culture, the mind and the body, the rational and the sensual. These memories are constructed out of the discourses and the culture in which I have lived; they draw from my life as a student, as a woman, as an artist-dancer, and as an educator-artist. I believe that they provide a depth and richness that allows the reader to become aware of the struggles and dialogue between my "felt" experiences and "reasoned" understandings. They are not only intended to be illustrative of a process, but also of the deeper connections between how one thinks and how one lives. The attempt here is to focus on particular situations in my own life so as to rediscover the sensual texture of these moments and situations. It means attempting to return to the past as a stranger, to recall and reassess personal history; and out of this, to demonstrate what it might mean to engage in a process of critical reflection that is centered on the body as a site of knowing and the source of self and social understanding. Out of this work I have been developing a curriculum approach that combines personal narrative with social critique using reflections on body memories to produce a language of cultural awareness. It is an approach that attempts to integrate critical pedagogy and feminist concerns and recognize the body as the central focus of the way the self is constituted in the world. I will return to this process in the conclusion.

What follows is a selection from the narratives of this memory-work. I begin with schooling.

Reflection One. The Body in the Hidden Curriculum

> So organized was the room I entered, everything had a place. Somehow it made me experience my own body as only an added clutter to the room. I wasn't sure if I had dressed carefully enough. Maybe

some hair was sticking out as it had a tendency to do when I had gone to bed the night before with it wet from bathing. So organized was the room, I couldn't decide where it was that I was suppose to be. Directed by the only figure who gave out firm and concise orders, the two of us my mother and I settled into two small chairs at the back table.

I partially sat down, meaning that even though I relented to the placement I continually rotated in the chair turning my body right and left trying to attend to the commotion of the other small figures entering into the room. I watched the procession. Each took a place. There was a one-way traffic pattern—entering. This process seemingly went on forever. As I became disinterested in the foregoing process, I began to "take in" my surroundings. The neatness and orderliness of it was strange to me. The room smelled old; somehow I knew that we weren't the first to experience this space. There persisted a feeling of oldness with the orderliness. I remembered my older brother's and sister's stories of school and how they had described the daily episodes between the teacher and the students around issues of discipline and control. How many children had wiggled, twisted, and turned in this seat before me? How many had been told to "stay in your seats until I tell you that you can get up.'"? I felt the smoothness left in the bottom of the chair from motion confined to it.

The longer I sat the more I began to feel the tension being produced by my desire to move around and explore. The more I became aware and concerned with the large looming figure who had strange powers over me, I began to feel myself become associated with all the small things in the room. I learned not be "out of place," never to touch anyone or anything unless directed to do so. It was like a waiting room but you didn't know what you were waiting for. I began to feel held in place by the walls, ceiling, floor, and the single door. Confined to the chair, my project became to escape it.

Over time the room took on a new meaning. It became a world. In that world, I took on a different identity. I became a student. There sandwiched between two others at a table of eight, I began to be something and someone else. And I wasn't sure of either. At that table I felt both ownership and a solidarity with my group. Yet I also had to compete with them to be the quietest, neatest, best-behaved student in order to gain the prizes of going for snack, dusting the erasers, leading the lunchroom line, or being praised by the teacher.

Above all else I learned I had to take care of myself first.

I suffered the confinement of that middle seat, in the second table along the side wall. My body manifested the bruises. The seating assignment filtered through every activity—the reading circle, the lunchroom seating, lining up for recess, drinking water, going to the bathroom, bus lines, and library trips. Throughout the school day I was presented with the task of having my body in a particular space in a particular way. I learned in multiple ways to maintain my body: face front; sit quietly; stay in line; raise my hand; not to look out the windows or door; not to talk, sing or make noises; not to run on the playground; and above all else, remain in my seat. Compressed, repressed, and controlled, the shared space between me and that room became a symbol of a situation that held unredeemed promises of pleasure, fun, and the excitement of exploration. *"Held" is the crucial word.* For they were held and allocated as a means to ensure conformity. If we could walk in a straight line to the lunchroom, we could have an afternoon story; if we put our things away quietly, we could have an extra five minutes of recess; if we finished our work without talking, we could paint, draw, or color. Every act became a bargain.

My urge to explore, discover, play and imagine, so well developed outside of school, became my enemies in school. "She" will let me know when, where, how, and with what I will be allowed to encounter this place, this enclosed room, where my public-education experiences began with the confining of my body—my spirit. Somewhere inside of me I felt the split begin.

The purpose of this retrospection is to bring to consciousness the process of self-formation through a narrative that allows the "embodied ideology" to speak. The attempt to uncover the multilayered meanings can best be understood through the work of those (such as Michael Apple, Jean Anyon, Peter McLaren, William Pinar, David Purpel, and others) who have examined the notion of a "hidden curriculum" in the schooling process. Realized within this work is a conceptualization of school as a place that produces and reproduces the social, economic, and political values of the dominant ideology. These values are transmitted through the day-to-day interactions, structures, and environment of schooling. Perhaps most importantly, educational institutions have as their goal the production of a labor force that can service and provide labor for the capitalist economic system.

Valerie Suransky, in her research concerning the schooling of preschool children, emphasizes the relationship between the industrialization of America and its public schools as one that produces students who "conform to the needs and expectations of the corporate and technocratic world." She writes:

The social landscape of the classroom, with an emphasis on discipline, punctuality, acceptance of authority, and accountability for one's world, replicated the social relations of the work place, facilitating an early acculturation to the social division of labor, thereby reproducing the class structures which mass education supposedly diminishes. (1983, p.136)

Developing alongside of this educational project of supplying a workforce based on class divisions was the "idea" of childhood tied to a technological ideology and what Giroux has called a "culture of positivism." The effect on schooling was the constant preoccupation with management, behavioral and instructional objectives, tracking, standardized testing, cost-benefit analyzes, and criteria of performance. It became a model that objectified, separated, and alienated the child from its own subjectivity through a process that, as Suransky argues, in its obsession with conformity and nonauthentic modes of being, "strips the self." Studies of the hidden curriculum have pointed to the denial of body needs—the separation of work and play, of school and life, of school knowledge and personal knowledge. These studies make clear how schooling represses creativity and imagination, produces alienation from feeling, and generates dehumanizing restrictions on physical movement. This takes place within the controlling phenomenon of time, the ever-present force of competition and success, and the incessant demand for obedience to authority. All of these foster what Suransky terms "nonauthentic modes of being."

Play is the child's praxis upon the world. Through play, children restructure, invent, create, and transform the given reality. Through play, the child's body becomes the mediator for her or his creative and agentic powers. Within schooling, however, the body of the child is the object of a curriculum that denies creative and imaginative powers. For to play, imagine, create, fantasize, explore, discover, or show curiosity threatens the structured landscape that is physically and psychically geared to minimize change. Repression, conformity, and sometimes resistance become the necessary mode of being for the child.

A specific social reality emerges, expressing a distinct set of social relations and assumptions about the world, and how one lives in that world. The child learns these in that which is most visibly controlled—the body. Therefore, the effects of such a process come to be associated, in the early years, in the way curriculum is geared to "body management." Jane Roland Martin (1985) has shown how this process is connected to an education that separates mind and body, and therefore diminishes our sense of the latter. Martin writes that "there is no place for education of the body, and since most action involves bodily movement, this means there is little room in it for education of action" (p. 73). Martin defines our liberal notion of education as developing, not the mind as a whole, but only the rational mind. The effect is a "disembodied" mind where reason keeps feeling and emotion under tight control. The result is "mindless bodies," bodies unfeelingly doing a job. In this model, feeling and emotion have no place. To accommodate such a model, students must alienate themselves from their own bodies—that which mediates their experiences and provides them with knowledge of the relationship between self and world.

Michael Apple and Nancy King in an article titled "What Do Schools Teach?" (1983, pp. 82-99), argue that the child's body becomes the crucial reminder of the immense gap left in an educational theory, theory that too often forgets the primacy of experience in the process of learning and that all knowledge is body-mediated knowledge. In order to critically reflect upon matters of pedagogy and the process of education, we must remember to include the somatic nature of learning and especially its early effects on the bodies of young children.

Reflection Two. Dance Class: Searching for Home

> Stand parallel. Roll down for eight, hang eight counts, demi-plie four counts, straighten, slowly roll up eight, releve four, lift both arms, rising from the side, plie and straighten. Breathe. Again. Head drops first, feel each vertebra as you slowly roll down. Sink into your plie, release your head, enjoy the release, keep your rotators engaged.

Make it flow. Be continuous, no stops, energy out the top of your head and down into the floor, expand, open up your back. Now in second position.

The first moments in dance class are for a recentering of mind and body; a pulling together of yourself, leaving outside everything that is "outside"—your life. The intention is to bring to the present a body in space and in motion which creates dance in time. Thought cannot wander; breathe deeply and fully; awaken yourself to your total presence. As class continues, tightened muscles give way to new directions altering patterns of movement. The overall feeling is of control, strength, and power.

I have prepared myself beforehand for dance. The leotard must be lightweight—preferably nylon or cotton, footless Danskin tights, and loose clothing as outerwear. There is always some extra covering for the body in case I feel that there is some part of my body which needs extra coaxing for "warming up" (a term that signifies to the dancer that the body has been sufficiently prepared to dance). Dancers spend the larger part of class in a warm up and in activities that strengthen muscles. Strategically, dancers attack "tight" muscles before class begins—rolling, swinging, pointing, flexing, dropping, turning, twisting, opening—doing whatever has been devised as a personal routine and ritualistically undertaken to prepare their body for class.

I prepare by lying on my back. I feel the presence of my body there on the floor. My total attention is to what I feel in my body in that space at that time. Each movement has been developed to help me feel my body—arms, legs, feet, hands, shoulders, lower and upper back, stomach, neck, head, and the connecting joints between them. I move to feel the muscles' resistance to the movement and their eventual giving into the movement. It is a double use of gravity. The floor beneath me becomes my grounding. I learn to work with it, the giving and resisting. Between them is where movement is found. In this state of being—a reality that incorporates restraint and freedom—there remains a constant grounding. The more strongly I feel my connectedness to the floor, the more stability I have, and the more security I have for moving.

> Grounding requires choice and responsibility. I must make a
> decision, a commitment to my grounding with a strength that will
> hold me in place. It is the strength of the commitment that will allow
> me the freedom to move with conviction. To dance fully there can be
> no holding back on either this commitment or the movement. To
> dance fully is to not withhold. To dance fully is to feel myself "alive"
> full of life. This is why I dance. My own grounding is felt in my "gut."
> It is from here that I feel centered. I experience dance from my cen-
> ter out. I can rise, lift, arch, turn, spiral, leap, reach, contract, and open
> from my body. With time through movement, energy is produced, or
> captured, and made to dance. It is for me "Eros," or life energy.
> Thinking and being become one when I dance. No longer are there the
> distinctions of mind and body. There is instead only being. When I am
> dancing nothing else exist for me. Space, time and energy—that
> which makes up dance—is made concrete by my body. I feel the sig-
> nificance of my own existence, which is deemed necessary for the
> dance to exist.

The experience of dance, described by a locating of self in time
and space, can appear to resist the fragmentation and alienation
so painfully present in the postmodern world. The dance experience can become a search for identity in a situation that appears
to offer a reconnection of mind and body through self-referencing
in time and space. The dance class for many dancers represents
"home"—one that becomes a site of a partial resistance to preset
identifications and preset placements in the existing social world.
There is here the rejection of a life that separates mind and body,
thought and feeling, creativity and existence. It is a search for
intimate connections between self and being, between self-consciousness and the act of living. The subject is offered an assum-
able identity in the dance class as that of a dancer who appears to
transcend the limitations and pain of the everyday world.

Unfulfilled potentiality is an essential part of being a dancer,
many times felt as a drive to perfection. One is constantly challenged, to struggle and achieve control over one's own body in
movement. For many it becomes a total commitment to "be per-
fect." There are classes every day, and rehearsals and perfor-
mances at night. The dancers separate themselves from the social

world in their need to "be in being." Eric Fromm (1966) describes this act of grasping the world through separation.

> Neither possession, nor power, nor sensuous satisfaction...can fulfill man's desire for meaning in his life; he remains in all this separate from the whole, hence unhappy. Only in being productively active can man make sense of his life, and while he thus enjoys life, he is not greedily holding on to it. He has given up the greed for having, and is fulfilled by being; he is filled because he is empty; he is much, because he is little. (p. 29)

The dancer's life is realized only during the time when one is dancing. John Berger (1984), as previously discussed, notes that this is a denial of time. Experiences that defy time create an illusion of existence without past and future, and without social connections. In this context of "unreal" time, the body/subject assumes an ephemeral existence. Indeed, the dancer constantly faces the possibility of her own effacement. Her existence is erased at the end of each dance. At each performance she is born, lives, and dies. Fredric Jameson refers to this as "the hysterical sublime."

> [I]t is the self that touches the limit; here it is the body that is touching the limits, "volatilized," in this experience of images, to the point of being outside of itself, or losing itself. (cited in Stephanson, 1988, p. 30)

Existence here is reduced to an instant of time in a most intense final punctual experience. It is, as Berger understands, a kind of nonhumanist experience of limits beyond which the subject gets dissolved.

The body for the dancer mediates the expectations and possibilities of becoming subjects of her or his world. Yet these can only be illusions of the unrealizable promises of liberation. For the dancer finds identity in the dance studio; an identity that cannot be carried into the life-world outside the studio. There is instead only the pretense of a subjectivity that can escape the fragmentation of its social being through the masculinized and commodified world of dance.

Reflection Three. Woman as Body

There is never a moment that I am without body, with the exception of sleep. And I'm not sure of even that. It's a nagging presence of what has been, what could be, and what will never be. My body—hair, skin, shape, size, smell—is a constant reminder of who I am as connected to what I appear to be in cultural terms.

Under stressful life conditions my face "breaks out"; when the time between dance classes is too long, my thigh muscles relax; when I change my dancing schedules, my metabolism slows down and inevitably within a week I have gained five more pounds. Every year my body tells me I'm aging—grey hair, dropped breasts, everything seems to be releasing to the pull of gravity, leaving drooping and dangling flesh. I know at all times what my physical appearance is.

Every day there is an examination to see where I am; that is, what appearance I have. From my memory of that perceived state of appearance comes my state of being. My psychological constitution is closely tied to the way I feel about my appearance. Questions concerning dress command the beginning of each day. The questions are very complex and demand a sophisticated response.

In the modern world many women play a double standard, I feel the pressure to conform to this double standard, creatively "pleasing myself" and dressing for comfort, while at the same time wanting to appear casually sexy, yet wholesome. My mind and body react—are the clothes I am wearing both attractive and comfortable? Attractive here meaning the materials being made out of natural fibers; and stylish but not trendy. They must pass several other "dressing" tests. Are they sensual to both feel and see, yet not blatantly sexy? Do they looked to be creatively put together in a sophisticated manner, yet retain an appearance of an "effortless creation?" Are the colors good for my skin tone? The "proper" clothes must also be chosen for a specific occasions: linen and silk blazers for cultural events; jeans for when one wants to express that "I still have a great body, like to have fun, and am somewhat rebellious; t-shirts for youth; sweats for that 'I'm serious about the shape of my body and I work at it'; wool for professional work; short dresses, baggy pants, or high heels for playtime such as going out to eat, dance, or to the theater; and cotton clothes and flat shoes for travel." These allude to only some of the typical standards for women's dressing, and they only speak to outerwear. There is at least as much, if not more concern with underwear, ranging from silk "teddies" to French-cut cotton undies. Colors, cuts, and fabrics provide an endless array of combinations that change with seasons and style over longer periods of time. Yesterday polyester was in vogue; today it is lycra.

Are the accessories such as earrings, shoes, scarves, bracelets, necklaces, and pens appropriately selected in relationship to gain the "total look"? Hair is also treated as an accessory. There remains a constant struggle: should I cut, perm, or color? what is the right length, shape and texture? how can I achieve the right amount of "mussiness" and have it still appear as if it is natural? Makeup presents the task of wearing it to appear as if you are not wearing it, but look so attractive naturally.

The amount of time and energy women expend on the appearance of the body is enormous. In such a culture where appearance is so tied to self-worth, women are constantly caught in a vicious circle. Vicious is the social reality in which the lives of women are consumed by the demands of appearance on their life energies. There is no way out. The body's appearance is equivalent to the signification of woman. This significance is manufactured desire, based upon the pleasures of appearance; that is, being "happy" with how one looks under the gaze of the dominant male aesthetic. Yet, John Berger (1984) argues, it is happiness to be achieved through a kind of functional gratification that can never be reached. Berger reveals the complexities and contradictions women are faced with when trying to achieve a sense of happiness through an aesthetic of appearance.

> Human happiness is rare. There are no happy periods, only happy moments. But happiness is precisely a generalized pleasure. And the state of happiness can be defined by an equation whereby, at that moment, the gift of one's well being equals the gift of existence. Without a surplus of pleasure over and above functional gratification, such well-being could not exist. (1984, p. 70)

Not only are women trapped by an aesthetic of appearance, they must also contend with an ideology that suggests freedom in terms of having a choice of "choosing their appearance." Understandably, the choosing of an image that directs how your being is perceived is not to be confused with the real freedom of choosing how you want to live. The former means to choose from a range in which identities (particularly female identity) can be re-made and re-presented, and be "made-over." The illusion of freedom must not be confused with the liberation from the actual constraints and limitations of our real conditions of existence. The positioning of women's bodies in society as objects of display and of identity gives us the apparent freedom of a world in which the self can be continuously repositioned, resituated, and reinvented. This freedom to choose self-identity is always circumscribed by the male gaze, which controls most of the public, as well as the private domain. It is a false perception of freedom. Women's bodies are channeled into the masculine domain of abstract sexuality and alienated sensuality.

Reflection Four. A Prejudice towards Difference

> There is something they know in their bodies. There is something they experience with their extra weight, their fat, that I don't. My body feels a repulsion to their heaviness, largeness, looseness. I watch in disgust as they maneuver, calculating aisle widths, chair size, furniture strengths. Folds of flesh hangs from chins, arms and bellies.
>
> I feel the weight of the loose, fat-filled skin. A churning in my stomach and the rising of a bile taste in my throat is my visceral response to the sight of them. I can't even fool myself about this prejudice. I can't say my feelings come from concern about their health or psychological well-being. The sight of their unkempt, seemingly uncared for bodies surely projects my powerful ambivalence towards my own body, which requires a constant maintenance of weight and shape.

Fatness, we are made to believe, is a physical sign of nature out of control. It is a perception that is surely rooted in man's fear of nature, and the consequent need to have power over it. The masculine determination to take control of nature is re-expressed in terms of corporeal shaping: "well built," "stacked," "shapely," "nice size," "well proportioned"—all capture a language that reflects the neurotic need to identify things in relation to size and therefore the ability to control. ("Don't take on more than you can handle" "Take things in hand" "You need to get control of yourself" "Get a hold on the situation" "Get on top of things")

This fear of nature projected onto the body becomes emblematic of the controlling relationship between man and nature (Haug, 1987). The relationship is perceived not in terms of intimacy and connection; rather it emphasizes an assumption of the self's control over nature, and therefore over our bodies. To appear to be physically "out of control" of your body—to deviate from the socially predetermined norms—is judged in moral terms. Consequently, how one appears physically implies how one's dignity is judged. "Letting her body go" is understood as an expression of bad character. "Not taking care of yourself" is an expression of moral irresponsibility. The dilemma we face is between a question of health and a question of a morally defined aesthetics (Ehrenreich, 1992).

Haug (1987) captures in her work the relationship between how we verbally describe people and our moral judgement of them. Since the 1960s the moral consequences of fatness have intensified, especially around a discourse of abuse that condemns us through what appears to be self-inflicted wounds to the body (e.g., in overeating, lack of exercise, etc.). "Being fat," "having a tummy," "carrying extra weight," and are understood as "achievements" of our character—something that we are actively doing, or have done, and for which we must therefore take responsibility. There can be no denial of the overriding effects of the appearance of women's bodies on their lives in this culture (e.g., "You can never be too thin, or too rich"). My own verbal description is a painful one. Yet it provides a powerful example of the oppressive culture in which I live. This example of embodied prejudice signifies the unacceptable nature of difference in this culture. "What is the loathing of difference that lives there?" It is a way of viewing that separates rather than unites. Audre Lorde urges each one of us to ask ourselves. "As women we have been taught to either ignore our differences or to view them as causes for separation and suspicion rather than as forces for change" (1983, p. 99). Lorde reminds us that without community there is no liberation, but community must not mean the shedding of difference, nor the pretense that difference doesn't exist. The inability to recognize the separating power behind society's definitions of "acceptable" women ensures the dehumanizing force found in the discourse of sameness. The denial of difference is the denial of reality, of the actual conditions in which we live. Our bodies—black, female, old, fat, poor, abused, differently able—tell us of difference, and they tell us of sameness. We are women who must emancipate themselves through, as Lorde argues:

> the need and desire to nurture each other...and it is within that knowledge that our real power is rediscovered. It is this real connection which is so feared by a patriarchal world. For it is only under a patriarchal structure that maternity is the only social power open to women. (pp. 98-99)

There are differences among women, and these differences can either separate or educate. Making the personal become political begins with a knowledge and acceptance of difference, and is the foundation for a vision for political action concerned with social justice and human liberation.

Reflection Five. Life against Death

> I created ridges by pressing the de-elasticized skin.
> Amazed I sat for a time that seemed to last for hours.
> Watching, feeling, pressing this old blue-veined, white skin.
> My small hands worked over hers.
> Pressing ridges and watching them disappear as they sunk back into their covering.
> Sometimes I could get as many as three ridges at a time,
> before one would slowly and completely disappear.
> She sat silently. There was only the sound of the clock,
> marking the time of days forever ticking.
> By the window, I kneeled, reaching her knees with my chest,
> fascinated by the feel of her skin as it rested on her hand,
> on the arm of the chair in the afternoon sun.

In my visit as a young child to an elderly neighbor woman's home, recounted above, I learned early that the body marks the time of life. Etched in the facial lines and marked by the flaccid skin are the experiences of a life; pain, joy, anger, pleasure, concern, have all seeped into the flesh representing a knowing through living. The soft, tight, and unmarked skin of our early years inevitably grows older and becomes marked with these life experiences. The body, as nothing else, ages with life. Unlike the airbrush images found in the media, which deny even the possibility of life experience, imperfect faces and bodies compel us to note the impressions of life inscribed on the flesh. They make present for us the passing of time. They mark for us what we fear most: the finality of death. The time when the body ceases to live. In modernity we cover over, fill out the lines, and evade the questions that are prompted by facing our own temporality.

Norman Brown postulates a theory for the denial of death in modern cultures (Balbus, 1982). He argues that the transmutation of the death instinct resurfaces in human behavior in two distinct, perverse, and destructive ways; in our relationship to nature and in sexual repression, the denial of our own bodies. The denial, according to Brown is, equivalent to the denial of death. The refusal to accept human mortality is comparable to the refusal of bodily pleasures that ends with the domination of nature. Isaac Balbus explains Brown's theory.

> Our bodies, as the living reminder of our mortality, must be repressed, forgotten; the transformation of the polymorphous perversity of the infant into the narrow, genitally concentrated sexuality of the adult not of the "outside" world but rather the child who cannot tolerate death: the inability to die and sexual repression are the two unique and related "privileges" of the human animal. We rise above ourselves, in short, in order to rise above death; the result is a deadening of our bodies. (Balbus, 1982, p. 294)

The effort to deny the passing of time, to become immortal, is the denial of dependence on the past, on tradition. This denial of the past and projection into the future always places one in the state of becoming. To always be in a mental state projected toward future, is also to be in a process that depends upon the escape from one's existence in the world. Simply stated, this means an "instrumental" attitude towards life that stipulates war against death. In so doing, our consciousness is preoccupied with the task of avoiding the past (history) and the present (reality). In the avoidance, life is lost. The instrumental mode wins out as one tries to constitute one's immortality through a constant and obsessive envisioning of one's future life. The present becomes only means for future living. Brown defines this consciousness where

> man is always trying to secure a spurious and delusive immortality for his acts by pushing his interest in them forward into time, in short, this is the time (consciousness) of the human being whose preoccupation with the future in the name of the (unconscious) drive to negate past prevents him from living in, and enjoying, the present. (cited in Balbus, p. 298)

Brown argues that a transformed consciousness of death requires a transformed body; a liberation of the body that would enable the "resurrection of the body" (p. 299). By embracing one's mortality one is able to embrace one's own flesh. Brown calls it a reversal of the instrumental relationship to death, and thus to nature. Balbus comments upon Brown's theory: "Only the individual who truly loves his (and other's) body can establish a loving but not self-abnegating, intimate yet autonomous, relationship with the body of nature" (p. 300). There are the inseparable connections among the acceptance of death, the celebration of the body, and the ability to live fully in the present. Unlike the instrumental mentality, the post-instrumental individual will be able to engage in present work with spontaneity and joy. The activity in which such liberated, eroticized individuals engage, vis-a-vis nature, can only be called "play." Only if Eros—as the life instinct—can affirm the life of the body can the death instinct affirm death, and in affirming death, magnify life.

Reflection Six. Touching

> There is nothing more real than being touched. It confirms our existence as something concrete. To be physically touched and spiritually touched both repairs and makes us whole again. The feeling of "com-

pleteness," the feeling of "oneness," the feeling of "relatedness," the feeling of "fullness" are all evoked as I am re-embodied by the touch of other.

I remember the warmth and strength I receive in that touch from another. I am able to release the barrier of protection I have surrounded myself with—words, clothes, books, work, degrees. My flesh becomes soft. My being is released to explore and know those precious moments when I seek the comfort that surrounds and embraces my femaleness, my presence as woman.

I am reminded of the masculine part of me as I experience your strength and groundedness in the world. You remind me of my own vulnerability, and with it the possibility for trust; you remind me of the pain and delight that bind relationships; you remind me of my intellectual self that has suffered the stunting from invalidation; you remind me of the possibility for self-transcendence as I come to care about other; you remind me of the ecstatic feelings held inside me; you remind me in your touch of the solidarity felt between two people in relationship; you remind me of the inseparability of love and justice.

So close were our bodies. We had fallen asleep knowing the warmth of another when lying together. There was a silence and separation only our bodies could fill. The fluidity of our beings seem to mix in the early morning hours. We seem to come to a state of pure existence. It is a time between being conscious and unconscious. Barriers have slipped away in the night as we release ourselves from protective coverings.

Naked we touch. The presence of life is captured in those few brief moments when we touch with love and allow another to experience what we keep most hidden and protected in our bodies—our hearts.

Relationships among women and men, women and women, men and men, parent and child, people of color and other races, old and young, healthy and diseased, human to earth, human to any other living thing, requires the ability to distance oneself, "to see" differences, and the ability to understand sameness, "to feel" relatedness. The important point is the communal knowing through our sensuality. Beverly Harrison notes the relationship between knowledge and sensuality: "all knowledge, including our moral knowledge, is body-mediated knowledge. All knowledge is rooted in our sensuality. We know and value the world, if we know and value it, through our ability to touch, to hear, to see.

Perception is foundational to conception" (1981, p. 36). Our power, all power, is rooted in feeling. What we perceive, think, conceive are all dependent upon sensuality. Feeling through our bodies mediates the knowledge as it connects us to the world. Harrison suggests that when we cannot feel we lose our connection to the world. If feeling is damaged, hardened, or cut off, our ability to reason, to image, or to act in the world is impaired. With the loss of feeling, of connection, of relatedness, we lose the capacity to conceive, value, or act as moral agents in the world. Harrison argues, "Failure to live deeply in "our bodies, ourselves" destroys the possibility of moral relations between us" (p. 13). Feelings, however, as Harrison suggests, are not an end in themselves. The attempt is not to get one "to feel more," or "feel better," or to "feel happier." Again we are reminded that the question is not "how I feel" but "what do I do with what I feel." Harrison points to the major source of rising moral insensitivity as one that is derived from being out of touch with our bodies. We have learned to live so much in our heads that we can no longer feel connectedness to other living things. It is a radical act of love that is needed—expressing human solidarity and bringing mutual relationship to life—to do justice.

It is, as Sharon Welch (1985) terms it, a poetics of revolution where there is the acceptance in living a paradoxical tension. This tension expresses the fragile balance between "absolute commitment" to what one feels is right and just, and "infinite suspicion" of those feelings or beliefs, allowing for challenges and modifications to avoid moral imperialism or triumphalism (p. 91). It is a discourse that speaks to our desire for wholeness, mutuality, and self-transcendence. Dorothee Soelle references those aspects of both the Jewish and Christian traditions that recognize the interconnection of loving and knowing in honor of our need for wholeness. She writes, "In the Hebrew Bible the verb to know has two different meanings; one refers to perceiving and understanding, the other to sexual intercourse" (Soelle & Cloyes, 1984, p. 147). Soelle brings together sexuality and intellectuality. She suggests that if we apply the cognitive connotations of the verb "to know" to our sexuality, then to know someone means being aware of the other, observing and recognizing who he or she is, and experiencing the many facets of the beloved's personality (p. 147). In severing our carnal and emotional desires from the desire to know, our knowledge of the other diminishes and becomes passionless.

Historically it has been man's prerogative to split off affection from lust, to perpetuate the mind/body split, in order to control and manipulate his own manifestations of his separated being. "Oneness" and "relatedness" give way to separations and abstractions. Yet Soelle calls for women not to simply adopt patriarchal sexual mores in an attempt to overcome inequality. She suggests one must stay close to the voice inside that calls for wholeness. There is a need for unity of the agentic and the responsible found in social relationships. Reflection on human sexuality is incomplete without attention to its sociopolitical dimension. Soelle calls this dimension of our sexuality "solidarity." To love more is to know more of our partner and of our human community. Eros and agape rejoin when ecstatic feelings in love heighten our awareness of the violence that imprisons others and denies them life's fullness (Soelle). Love is not separable from justice. In concluding, Soelle gives powerful metaphors for "making love" and "making justice":

> The drive to make love and to make justice should be one; it will become one the more we overcome the current split between private and public life.... But if our embodiment in lovemaking does not move us beyond the acute, narrow joys and sorrows of our own bodies to the body politic, then it has not gone far enough. (pp. 152-153)

Life is a principle, not a thing. The body is not life, it is a manifestation of life. To touch and be touched holds memories of human connection. Loving touch bears with it the hope for a just community. With love we affirm and are affirmed. In the sociopolitical struggle against death from hunger, disease, exploitation, war, destruction of the earth, and against hopelessness there is a great and growing need for our capacity to become "body-full" with love.

Conclusion

People stand before suffering like those who are color-blind, inca-
pable of perception and without sensibility. (Soelle, 1975, p. 38)

Such blindness, the liberation theologian Dorothee Soelle
suggests, is only possible in a society that is unable to perceive
suffering, not only one's own, but especially the suffering of others. It is a kind of "freedom" from suffering that levels out one's
sensual life—that is, a life in which feeling is either forgotten or
denied. This desensitization process permeates our human connections and provides the apathetic condition which Soelle
claims so characterizes our culture. Soelle describes pathy as "a
form of the inability to suffer." Apathy, as a state of being, can
only be present with the repression of one's feelings of connections to oneself, others, and the world.

Recent surveys have made clear that an apathetic consciousness, as a way of relating to life experiences, is dominant within
the culture of America's young. This consciousness has within it a
corresponding absence of passion for life, and commitments felt as
compassionate human beings. It is this apathetic condition that
frames our emotional life and sensual existence. Life energies
become congealed to create the sense of a "reality" where there are
"no disruptions," "no involvements," and "no sweat." To "feel," to
resolidify human connections, means to be willing to struggle. To
do so represents a movement of resistance against passionless
lives, against alienation, indifference, repression, and separation.
In such a movement, we may again become grounded. The body
experiencing deeply is recognized as that which makes possible
the reconnection to our own lives, and others; that which makes
possible the recovery of our humanity from its apathetic condition.
It is the body that carries knowledge of a life; the memories of
love, joy, softness, warmth, laughter, touch, and the human desire
for freedom. It is the material foundation upon which the desire for
human liberation and social transformation rests.

References

Anyon, J. (1997). *Getto schooling: A political economy of urban educational reform*. New York: Teachers College Press.

Apple, M., & King, N. (1983). What do schools teach? In D. E. Purpel & H. Giroux (Eds.), *The hidden curriculum and moral education* (pp. 82-99). Berkeley: McCutchen.

Balbus, I. D. (1982). *Marxism and domination*. New Jersey: Princeton University Press. Berger J. (1984). *And our faces, my heart, brief as photos*. New York: Pantheon Books.

Berger, J., & Mohr, J. (1982). *Another way of telling*. New York: Pantheon Books.

Bordo, S. (1990). Feminism, post modernism, and gender-scepticism. In L. J. Nicholson (Ed.), *Feminism/Postmodernism* (pp. 133-157). New York: Routledge.

Brodkey, L., Fine, M. (1988). Presence of mind in the absence of body. *Journal of Education, 170*(3), 84-99.

Corrigan, P. (1988). The making of the body: Meditations on what grammar school did with, to, and for my body. *Journal of Education*, 170(3), 142-161.

Eagleton, T. (1990). *The ideology of the aesthetic*. Cambridge: Basil Blackwell..

Ehrenreich, B. (1992, May/June). The morality of muscle tone. *Utne Reader,* 51, 65.

Fine, M. (1991). *Framing dropouts: Notes on the politics of an urban high school*. Albany: State University of New York Press.

Fromm, E. (1966). *Marx's concept of man*. New York: Ungar.

Giroux, H. (1985). Critical pedagogy, cultural politics & the discourse of experience. *Journal of Education*, 167(2), 22-41.

Giroux, H.A., & Simon, R.I. (1988). Schooling, popular culture, and a pedagogy of possibility. *Journal of Education*, 170(1), 9-26.

Greene, M. (1990, Spring). Multiple voices and multiple realities: A re-viewing of educational foundations. *Educational Foundations*, 5-19.

Hammer, R., & McLaren, P. (1989). Critical pedagogy and the postmodern challenge. *Educational Foundations*, 3(3), 29-62.

Harrison, B. (1985). *Making the connections*. Boston: Beacon Press.

Haug, F. (1987). *Female sexualization*. London: Verso.

Keleman, S. (1981). *Your body speaks its mind*. Berkeley: Center Press.

Lorde, A. (1983). The master's tools will never dismantle the master's house. In C. Morgan, & G. Anzaldua (Eds.), *The bridge called my back*. New York: Kitchen Press.

Martin, J. R. (1985). Becoming educated: A journey of alienation or integration? *Journal of Education*, 167(3), 71-84.

McDade, L. (1987). Sex, pregnancy, and schooling: Obstacles to a critical teaching of the body. *Journal of Education*, 169(3), 58-79.

McLaren, P. (1989). *Life in schools*. New York: Longman.

McLaren, P. (1988). Broken dreams, false promises, and the decline of public schooling. *Journal of Education*, 170(1), 41-65.

McLaren, P. (1988). Schooling the postmodern body: Critical pedagogy and the politics of enfleshment. *Journal of Education*, 170(3), 53-83.

Morrison, T. (1987). *Beloved*. New York: Knopf.

Pinar, W. (1981). Whole, bright, deep with understanding; Issues of qualitative research and autobiographical method. *Curriculum Studies*, 13(3), 173-188.

Pinar, W. (1978). Currere: Towards reconceptualization. In J. R. Gress & D. E. Purpel (Eds.), *Curriculum an introduction to the field* (pp. 526-545). Berkeley: McCutchen.

Purpel, D. E. (1988). *The moral and spiritual crisis in education*. Massachusetts: Bergin & Garvey.

Shapiro, H. S. (1991). The end of radical hope? Postmodernism and the challenge to critical pedagogy. *Education and Society*, 9, 2, 112-122.

Shapiro, H. S. (1989). Towards a language of educational politics: The struggle for a critical public discourse in education. *Educational Foundations*, 3(3), 79-101.

Sloterdijk, P. (1987). *Critique of cynical reason.* Minneapolis: University of Minnesota Press.

Soelle, D. (1975). *Suffering.* Philadelphia: Fortress Press

Soelle, D., & Cloyes, S.A. (1984). *To work and to love: A theology of creation.* Philadelphia: Fortress Press.

Stephanson, A. (1988). Interview with Fredric Jameson. In A. Ross (Ed.) *Universal abandon.* Minneapolis: University of Minnesota Press.

Suransky, V. (1983). Tales of rebellion and resistance: The landscape of early institutional life. *Journal of Education*, 165(2), 135-157.

Turner, B. (1984). *The body and society.* Oxford: Basil Blackwell.

Weiler, K. (1991). Freire and a feminist pedagogy of difference. *Harvard Educational Review*, 61(4), 449-474.

Weiler, K. (1988). *Women teaching for change.* Massachusetts: Bergin & Garvey.

Welch, S. (1985). *Communities of solidarity and resistance.* New York: Orbis Books.

CHAPTER FIVE

The Dancer's Life:
Existence and Transformation

Few people in education are formally charged with a concern for "educating" the body. Those who are include physical education teachers and teachers of dance. There is, in our schools, little notion of what East Europeans used to call "physical culture," that is a notion of corporeal development that was seen as part of an integrated approach to developing "the whole person." For the most part, physical education remains distinguished from (and subordinated to) development of the mind. Yet, dance and dance teachers find themselves located most often in the shadowy region of the arts where, in usually vague ways, aesthetic development is referred to as a matter of both heart and mind, body and intellect, and imagination and skill. Little work has been done to show how dancers come to understand their own peculiar location in the world—one that, as this chapter shows, positions them towards the culture in some very contradictory ways. An exploration of how these individuals think about their work and their lives might illuminate the larger contradictions of the culture as it relates to questions of body, knowledge, and meaning. As we will see here dance, like all aesthetic practices, struggles with its tendencies towards social critique and transformation, and its position as a peripheral, isolated, and alienating set of experiences.

Dialogue as Research
To dialogue with dancers is much like making a dance. As interviewer I came with the words like steps, putting them out there, letting the form of the questions shape to the form of the dancer.

They were questions I claim as mine in looking back at my own life as a dancer. I ask myself these questions in beginning this research: What is it that I want to inquire about? What is it that calls to me to be said? What is it that I hear, and what is it that I am silencing? All of these questions I referenced to dance— dance as a way of existence.

I discovered through this project the importance of knowing the questions. The search expanded to larger questions, "Why do we dance?" and "Why do we exist and how do we find meaning?" The dancer's life became the focal point of this research where I question, interpret, and try to reveal some aspects of the dancer's life. Here the dancer's life becomes emblematic of the search for grounding in the fragmented lives we live in contemporary society. Specifically, I discuss the loss of tension between a notion of "thrownness" in the Heideggerian sense and "authentic existence" in the Freireian sense; or the question of the relationship of the personal to the political. This discussion provides the ground for a critique of the social role artists play, and further how this social role, as understood and lived out, limits possibilities for both self and social transformation. In discussing how (women) dancers embody particular cultural or aesthetic codes and ideological structures, we come to understand how the body becomes a site for both subjugation and resistance.

I am interested in the way dancers make sense of their own existence; that is, how they reflect and interpret the existential dimensions of their lives as artists in contemporary society. I assume, with Merleau-Ponty (1994) the notion that the deeper we go into the individual's mind, the closer we get to the world. Yet I also wish to avoid the implicit dualism of Merleau-Ponty's knowing (where mind, not body, mediates the world). In trying to dissolve the dualism, I still find myself caught in a bifurcated language. Yet, I know of no other way to deconstruct it than to name it. By attending to embodied experiences—what the dancers "feel" in relationship to particular, and I believe, significant existential and critical questions—we can begin to develop a discourse that transcends the view of mind carried in, but separate from, the body.

The complication of avoiding dualistic language is further compounded by the peculiar and profound relationship of women to their bodies. In so many well-documented ways, women's connection to the world is defined and structured by the relationship of their bodies to the world. We must, therefore, turn from a discourse of "the mind in the body" to one where there is a "minding of the body." In this way we might give a better representation of what it means to live as a body/subject. In the case of dancers, who are women (as is the case in this study), there is an intensification of this phenomenon. For them, as we will see, the body not merely mediates the world, it "takes flight" as the vehicle through which transcendence, freedom, and meaning become experienced. In short, it grounds an ecstatic mode of being.

The three women I interviewed for the study were in a graduate dance program with an emphasis on modern dance. They had chosen dance as a profession and as a way of life. From the interviews, three key issues are discussed in this chapter: (1) the dancer as solitary individual; (2) the dance studio as home for the dancer; and (3) the body as the site of resistance and oppression. These issues concern the role of artists (dancers) and art in society, the search for home, and how the body/subject in dance offers a vision of another way of being. My own hopes in this research, which calls ultimately for the dancers to name their world, lie in John Berger's words "The naming of the intolerable is itself a hope" (1984, p. 18).

The Dancer as Solitary Individual:
Artist or Cultural Worker?

The dancer knows herself as a person on the fringes of society—a "social outcast." The artist, seen in this way, is the product of a particular period and set of social relations. Two crucial historical developments here are the rise of individualism with the development of industrial capitalism; and the separation of the artist from any particular social group or class, and therefore from any secure patronage (Wolf, 1981). Artists were left to struggle in the marketplace as art became a commodity. Modernity clothed artists in a garment of ultimate individualism.

The modernist's cry for absolute individual freedom, though a great step toward self-realization, implies a negative attitude toward society (Gablik, 1984). These connecting phenomena shape a kind of exaggerated individualism. Suzi Gablik notes, "We need not be Marxists to perceive the extent to which over-weening narcissism, compulsive striving, and schizoid alienation have become the dark underbelly of individual freedom in our society " (p. 32). This place of the artist in some state of hyper-individualism descends into an aesthetics of self, and also of a self-seeking.

When asked why dance is important to them, the intervie-wees answered in terms of personal fulfillment.

⌖ Dance is important because it has allowed me to do what I want to do...it gives me a vehicle to go beyond where I thought it was possible to go.

⌖ Dance is important because it gives you a sense of yourself.... It gives you a way of finding your place in the world.

Their words speak to finding identity, place, and the possibility of transformation. Implicit in their answers is a search for self in time and space, and the need to being located not only in a tem-poral space, but also in a personally transformational one. Yet, positioned on the margin of society, alienated from her social context, she experiences it alone, as a once-and-for-all solitary soul. Eliminated here is the possibility of any location, other than that of the alienated individual. The existential quest is a contra-dictory one, for both separation from the social and for location of oneself in the world. This fragmentation of the social and the personal mirrors the more general social life as a whole. The dancer experiences what Fredric Jameson (1983) calls the "mod-ern aesthetic sensibility" where time is separated from historical time and experienced overwhelmingly as a present or now time. This temporal breakdown echoes the schizophrenic existence of disassembled "nows." Reality, as such, can easily become unre-ality, yet with a heightened sense of aliveness.

≈Dance makes me feel alive...it gives me an awareness of my limitations. I guess it's an awareness of everything. Dance frightens me, being present at the time with others watching...but it makes me feel whole.

This aliveness, and the heightened perceptions felt when dancing, makes it difficult to question the disconnection to historical time. Dancers overlook the violence done to them, to their subjective experience, in their abstraction from the social context of their existence.

The dancer lives the life of alienation. She calls it home, denying the relationship between present, past, or future. Yet she continues to hold a belief about the potential to transcend this mode of existence. She speaks about dance as "a vehicle to go beyond."

≈ All art is an attempt to go further...into another place...to find the essence of what it is all about.

To "go beyond" is a statement rejecting the stasis of alienation and reclaiming the possibilities for human transformation. Her words speak to a commitment to meaningful existence, and to a resistance towards dehumanizing labor where her body is just another body; one where labor takes away creativity and imagination—indeed annihilates the body/subject. The dancer's alienation is a continuous struggle to hold the self together through separation from, and rejection of, contemporary life and alienating labor. Dance, then, becomes synonymous with hope.

≈ Dance has allowed my vision, ambitions, or ideals to match or fulfill them more than I ever imagined anything else, and has given me the opportunity to find a way of fulfilling ideals, and being able to expand ideas, not only about dance, but about life.

This hope is rooted in an awareness of incompletion, which moves the dancer into an existential search. It is a search for authentic existence through liberation, but one in which the dancer falls short. Paulo Freire, (1988) defines authentic liberation as calling for action and reflection of humans upon their world in order to transform it. For these women there is an understanding and affirmation of authentic existence where their work is connected to them in some meaningful way; where their passions, desires, and hopes are displayed in, with, and through their bodies; where passionate understandings are etched out on the space of the stage and intensely lived, even if only for an evening. The dancer feels the "lightness of being," though with a consciousness that hears the call to authentic, or meaningful existence. At the same time this consciousness remains ungrounded in the loss of the centrality of "being-with"—of being situated within society. This denial of being socially situated or bound is also the loss of historical connections and awareness. This loss in fact exacerbates the dancer's need for identity and for place. Lack of social consciousness, or rejection of social connectedness, hinders the knowledge of how social conditions affect, determine, and help to create their own existential crisis. The inability to understand their apparent positioning as asocial and ahistorical subjects relegates artists to the realm of ideological conformism. The world is seen as an arena only for the achievement of one's own success and satisfaction. "To the extent that an artist seeks only personal objectives, personal satisfaction, and self-aggrandizement," writes Suzi Gablik, " we cannot say that he fulfills any moral obligation (1984, p. 96). Yet these women, who may not have an articulated critical social theory for understanding their choices, do still speak in a critical language when discussing the possibilities for themselves and for their work. The two most spoken works were "commitment" and "strength":

≈ *What stands apart is their [artist] strength and commitment [disconnected from any institutions]...institutions feed them back into institutions.... They [artists] are prepared to explore their own being, rather than feeding other peoples'.*

She sees herself staying outside society in order not to be incorporated into institutional life. This place of resistance to adaptation to the social order is where she finds power, and where she constitutes her own vision of a meaningful life.

> *I'm really concerned about how people are going to overcome the threat of nuclear devastation...that motivates me three days a week.... The fact that I exist and that people will exist after me...if I can prevent that [disaster] from happening, that is what drives me to work, and inhibits my desire to have family. If I can't begin to find some power in my own work to make some kind of change, or some sense of satisfaction, then life is kind of meaningless. Why do we perform if it is not going to reach something?*

The key here is the contradiction—one is both outside the social context and, at the same time, has a desire to affect social change. This, in itself, is a defeat of the cynicism so often felt in modern society when one succumbs to the feeling of powerlessness. Gablik (1984) connects the desires of these dancers for meaningful existence to one which opposes helplessness and hopelessness. She states "succumbing to the feeling of powerlessness that makes it seem as if we are being dragged along in the wake of a system we cannot hope to challenge. To oppose this process—of resigning oneself to the fate of being helpless—is one of the crucial functions of the artist" (p. 101). Yet with the loss of grounding in the world, how can one begin to challenge the system within which it revolves?

The dancer's space is marked out within a realm of freedom demanding human dignity and non alienating work. This refusal is expressed by the dancers when talking about how they and their work are perceived.

> *Yes, I think of myself as an artist...[being an artist] means I really work hard at stuff no one else likes...an artist is someone who sees relationships, ponders things, tries to make sense of them, and works through an art form.*

⌐ *Dancers are other. We are in the "other" category. We're*
   allowed to be late, to be spacey, allowed a lot of other things
   because we are artists. [Also, we are] expected to be flam-
   boyant, eccentric, profound...certain things are expected.

Accepting the social position of isolation and of being outside the world, the illusion of the artist as someone who inhabits
a metaphysical domain remains. Labels such as "genius,"
"strange," "weird," "eccentric," "unreliable," frame both position
and identity. This oppressive designation of the artist is, at the
same, time coupled with a liberatory sign. For it can also be
understood as a sort of refusal of subjectivity from the "uncre-
ative, unimaginative and ungifted" notion of being human. The
question of how can one claim distance from "the world" and yet
remain committed in an existential and ethical sense is answered
in the work of Seyla Benhabib (1995).

> The vocation of social criticism might require social exile, for there
> might be times when the immanent norms and values of a culture are
> so reified, dead or petrified that one can no longer speak in their name.
> The social critic who is in exile does not adopt the "view from
> nowhere" but the "view from outside the walls of the city," wherever
> those walls and those boundaries might be. (p. 29)

It may be here, from the "walls outside the city," that the artist
can begin to transcend immediate reality. From here, as Herbert
Marcuse (1978) suggests, one can shatter the reified objectivity
of established social relations. This is where, Marcuse says, there
is the "rebirth of rebellious subjectivity" (p. 7). From here there
can follow a notion of art in which there is commitment to an
emancipation of sensibility, imagination, and reason. Here, aesthetic work becomes a vehicle for the recognition of the social
construction of reality and identity; to the estrangement of languages and images that makes visible the relationships we live—
those that are no longer, and those which do not yet exist.
   The artist's marginal place and romanticized identity hinders
any movement toward a notion of art which can transcend reali-

ty and shatter concepts of gender, class, race, sameness and difference, or even of art itself. Unfortunately, for the most part,
dance can best be described as an existential, individual rebellion
sealed within its own walls. It is a limited narcissistic rebellion.
As poignantly said by one dancer:

☞ *My work comes out of me...I often dance for myself.*

Home for the Dancer

Frames of reference for the artist are often defined in terms of
negatives: those experiences in which one feels dead. Death
becomes the determining factor to measure how one lives in time
(Arendt, in Young-Bruehl, 1982). In capitalist culture, which
abandons its claim to culture, life becomes nothing more than an
"Instant-Practice" (Berger, 1984). Modes of being and categories
of existence, which are defined in hopes of a transcendent life and
by the experience of a heightened sense of time, create a particular kind of "homelessness." Structured in an era in which there is
a "denial of history, the death of man, and the death of metaphysics" (Benhabib, Butler, Cornell, & Fraser), the contemporary
dance world for the dancer appears to offer a place, an alter of
sorts, to the desire for meaningful community—a shelter from the
ungrounded nature of human hope and possibility.

When the dancers were asked to reflect upon their sense of
home, they expressed an ambivalence toward their "dance
home." As earlier discussed, there was a concern for being
labeled by society in stereotypical ways such as, "elitist," "uppi-
ty," "snobbish," and "unreliable," whereas in the dance community they expressed a concern for dance closing in on itself—
where all concerns are about and for dance. Yet along with these
ambivalences, they spoke of the dance community as one that
offers identity and belonging, a sense of home.

☞ *I think there is community there. I don't feel a part of it...I feel
outside of it.*

The other two dancers described their sense of the dance community.

✒ *I don't think you can get away from community in the dance world.... Dance communities tend to be very closed.*

✒ *[I] very much so [feel a sense of community], in the smaller world [of dance]. People say hi. In the larger hierarchical dance, I am very aware of where I stand. I make a home in dance.*

The "dance" home has replaced the "family" home. Dance as a way of life takes precedence over all other life decisions.

✒ *Certainly I don't have family at the moment because of the work I've chosen to do.... I find it very difficult to ever think of family. My desire to fulfill whatever it is that dance offers is stronger than my need for family...having my own children I find hard to imagine.*

✒ *...in terms of my marriage I see it becomes a real problem. We have to face choices and make decisions based on, I want to perform then I want to teach.*

✒ *[The decision to have] children is another thing...I would never give up my dancing and I don't think I would give up my career. Don't ask me that question, it is scary...[dance] takes such dedication, it takes so much time it really hurts relationships, sacrificing...it takes precedence most of the time...it's who you are.*

The search for connection, for home in the world through dance, rejects the traditional notions of family and home. It carries with it the hope of completion, and compels the movement of returning to something only vaguely remembered, perhaps something imagined. Maybe only a childhood dream, or utopian cry, the search for completion and home. If not now, then in the future, where there is love uniting two displaced persons, and where home serves as the place for this hope of completion to reside.

In sensing these historical deaths, the dancers confront the Heideggerian notion of "thrownness." In dance they have come to find themselves in a world that appears to offer home, community, and the unification of self and desire. The self is held together through focusing on the body in dance; the dancers attempt to locate themselves concretely in time and space. The body dancing provides an image of the unification of self in time and in space. The dancer knows where the body is within defined spaces such as the studio or stage. The studio becomes the improvised home. These improvised dwellings, says John Berger (1984), are built "of habits, I think, of the raw material of repetition, turned into a shelter.... Home is no longer a dwelling but the untold story of a life being lived. At its most brutal, home is no more than one's name—whilst to most people one is nameless" (p. 64). The mortar that holds together the home is memory.

Dance and home becomes synonymous in meaning. For the dancer, they both speak to place. The home for dancers becomes the *place* to find the meaning of their existence:

> *If we are here to exist, it has to be rich and satisfying, and as meaningful as possible...I have to give purpose to that existence and that is why I work, why I dance, to give purpose to that existence.*

The chosen home of dance is a precarious one; one spoken of as not quite existing, one that floats, offering no significant grounding:

> *It's hard [being in dance] cause sometimes you feel like you're floating...I'm not going to hit the ground. You never know where you are.*

> *I think dance has a tendency to float somewhere about two inches above the ground.*

John Berger writes, "Nevertheless, by turning in circles the displaced preserve their identity and improvise a shelter" (p. 64). This provisional home, then, has a metaphysical quality. She—the dancer—feels outside of the "real" world, and left "floating out there" somewhere in dance. Is this floating symbolic of a will toward freedom? Is she escaping to find freedom in the space away from the world of rules and boundaries, away from the determinations of historically determined selves? As such, it fails to confront the constraints and pressures of the "lived-world," to insist on an emancipatory vision lived "at the heart of the real." Berger writes,

> the shelter of a home will not just be our personal names, but our collective conscious presence in history, and we will live again at the heart of the real.... Meanwhile, we live not just our own lives but the longings of our centuries. (p. 67)

The dancer's commitment to dance is a commitment to herself, but holds within it the profound longing of our time: a desire for home.

Body

> Their bodies bear their societies like stigmata.
> —Brian Fay

The body becomes the site for control and placement. Controlled bodies stand beside uncontrolled lives. The body is projected as a coherent image in time and space. The image is an illusionary representation of a nonexisting situation. It is an embodiment of an ideal that demands perfection. These women speak about perfection of their bodies as a repressive action.

> ✎ *The largest void in my life is perfection...because the body is involved it becomes even greater...dancing represses your body.*

⌇ *...being a dancer is never feeling like you are ever going to be good enough...you're never going to quite make it...there is no end, you know you can always get better but you know it is never good enough.*

⌇ *There are many times I feel repressed. The body itself can be confining and restricting. You can have ideas and images you can never fulfill.*

The body becomes thing—an object to be perfected. The knowledge of incompletion that kindles hope becomes entangled between the dancer and the perfected image. Hope is caught in a dialectic between thing and illusion. Distorted into an object, the body is one that is never quite good enough.

⌇ *I'm constantly, I'm not, I'm not, I'm not.*

The dancer's body appears to present the possibility that if one only works hard enough, one can reach beyond place. It appears as a lie. The dancing body does not show what the dancer lives. There is no connection between past and future. There is only an image taken out of time creating an image of an image. Berger (1982) speaks to the loss of time.

> Consequently the common experience of those moments which defy time is now denied everything which surrounds them. Such moments cease to be like windows looking across history towards the timeless. Experiences which prompt the term *for ever* have now to be assumed alone and privately. Their role has changed; instead of transcending, they isolate (p. 108).

If the dancer looks into the image, she can see the correspondence of her life to that of the postmodern world where we see a surfeit of anguish of isolation, alienation, and impermanence. Time-altered, the body-form is victimized as it slips away into an ephemeral existence. The dancer is constantly threatened with effacement, her existence erased at the end of each dance. At each performance she is born, lives, and dies. Fredric Jameson (1983) speaks of this hysterical sublimity: "It is the self that touches the limit; here it is the body that is touching the limits, 'volatilized,' in this experience of images, to the point of being outside of itself, or losing itself" (p. 38). It is a reduction of time to an instant in a most intense final punctual experience, but no longer a subjective experience connected to discursive meaning. On the contrary, it is a kind of an experience of limits, ungrounded, and one in which "you" get dissolved. This bodily-felt transcendence, isolated in the "now," makes impossible the kind of transcendence Sharon Welch (1985) calls for—one that is located in the historical, where memory is called upon to envisage an alternative future. When the dance no longer exists, where does the dancer reside?

Yet when dancing, the dancer feels freed, associating this feeling of aliveness with liberation. The body moving constantly rejects stasis (as if that were the real meaning of freedom).

ℑ Once you're in flight...there is a sense of boundlessness...and because [dance] really fires your imagination you can be anywhere in any place and you can dance and nobody can know what you are thinking.

The word "flight" takes on a double meaning here. Flight in dance is a sense of movement, that defies gravity. Another use of the word "flight" for women has been to describe an oppositional way of life. Helene Cixous (1980) delineates "flying" as a way for women to "mess up" the masculine order.

We've lived in flight, stealing away, finding, when desired, narrow passageways, hidden passovers. It's no accident women take after birds.... They go by, fly the coop, take pleasure in jumbling the order of space, in disorienting it, in changing around furniture, dislocating things and values, breaking them all up, emptying structures, and turning propriety upside down. (p. 167)

The dancer as woman steals away from the realm of masculine domination where woman has become man's property. Likewise the dancer as woman reclaims her body. Her bodily pleasures do not gravitate around male sexuality. These women speak about their bodies when dancing:

♂ *[Dancing] can be erotic, it's like making love to yourself. It is sensuous, a sensate thing.*

♂ *Yes, dance is erotic, sensual...I feel bodily pleasures, but seldom sexual.*

♂ *I can feel erotic when I'm dancing in a field with a band playing, not in class or on stage.*

Their bodies are self-referencing. Their passion for movement, for feeling alive, creates pleasure without mediation. They deny the censoring of the body; a body of female sensuality and erotic pleasure. They resist the objectification of the female body as an object for the male gaze, simply for male satisfaction, or as sexual object. Yet the confusion of sexual pleasure with eroticism is shown by these women when they talk about their sexual feelings when dancing:

♂ *I don't feel sexual, wait that's not fair, sometimes. I do, and I don't know where that comes from.*

♂ *I don't feel sexually aroused, but find that passion.*

♂ *I've never thought about it [performing] being sexual or erotic, but maybe it is like that.*

Perhaps I should state here that one of the dancers is married, another engaged, and the third involved in a heterosexual relationship. They do not deny their attraction to men, but struggle for their own bodily pleasures, and their own lives as women. In reclaiming the body, the dancer makes claims to her life told and understood through her experiences. Being a modern dancer can be a celebration of the body in its fullness; bodies sweat, legs open, women lift women, women lift men. As one dancer said, "It's equal-opportunity lifting." They fight back aggressively through dancing. They undo the female position of weakness and subordination. They speak through their bodies about female repression.

⋧ *Being a woman and the pressures I've always felt not to con-*
   form to be what women are suppose to be...I'm not going to
   conform, I'm not going to be some pretty young girl with her
   hair tied back with ribbons.

⋧ *I'm a feminist and I'm furious...the body [language] has been*
   clamped.

⋧ *If we somehow publicly show power and strength and sensu-*
   ality it's very negative. Even if we show true emotions other
   than this subservient kind of crap.

The modern dancer's body slashes, rolls, pulsates, and squats, producing images that defy the beautiful girl-dancer stereotype (a fairy like, virginal girl-woman found in many of the ballet roles) (Adair, 1992). The aesthetic of the beautiful is replaced in modern dance with what Marcuse (1969) calls the "imagery of liberation." It is here we can find the radical potential of dance. The dancer's body testifies to what is. The dancer's way of life preserves the struggle for freedom. She moves against body images that contain women; yet, paradoxically, she continues to be threatened by the prison house of dance's own limited aesthetic code.

Conclusion

Though often without great consciousness, the dancer resists and struggles against alienation, calling for a new sensibility: one that remembers the connection between human dignity and the will to freedom; one that questions a society that commodifies the female body and restricts the transformative power and vision of artists.

I began by stressing the importance of naming the intolerable by these dancers. The ability to name is linked to the ability to critically interpret and contextualize one's situation. Pedagogically, what I urge is that the dancer must, through this naming, bring the social situation to form so that the social context can be depicted; and so that the deep structure, as well as the surface, can be illuminated. Ultimately she needs to understand that personal liberation is inseparable from political liberation. What I will call an aesthetic existence (and here you will note I use the word aesthetic in a way that is different to its usual usage) implies both consciousness and conscience: the capacity to name and the commitment to an ethical vision. The aesthetic, as we have said before, is the region of feeling, that is, the body. My pedagogic interest (as I will show in the final chapter), is in bringing this region of feeling—the body/subject—into the context of an ethical vision concerned with understanding, naming, and transforming the world. Eagleton (1990) succinctly defines the double-edged possibility of the aesthetic described in this chapter.

> On the one hand, it figures as a genuinely emancipatory force—as a community of subjects now linked by sensuous impulse and fellow-feeling rather than by heteronomous law, each safeguarded in its unique particularity while bound at the same time into social harmony. The aesthetic offers the middle class a superbly versatile model of their political aspirations, exemplifying new forms of autonomy and self-determination, transforming the relations between law and desire, morality and knowledge, recasting the links between individual and totality, and revising social relations on the basis of custom, affection and sympathy. On the other hand, the aesthetic signifies what Max Horkheimer has called a kind of "internalized repression," inserting social power more deeply into the very bodies of those it subjugates, and so operating as a supremely effective mode of political hegemony. (p. 28)

Dance as an aesthetic existence calls for responsible choices within specific situations and depends on the recognition of the interdependence of self and other, individual and world. In bringing the artist to this place, she is freed to hear the call of human existence, to recognize that all choices are a part of creating humankind, and of creating the world in which we live. As Clarissa Estes (1992) writes:

> A whole psychology has to include not only body, mind, and spirit, but also, equally, culture and environ. And it is in this light, it must be asked at each level how it came to be that any individual woman feels she has to cringe, flinch, grovel, and plead for a life that is her own to begin with. (p. 240)

Suffering from the addiction of modern science, aesthetics became the study of sensuous perceptions as they affect individual feelings. What was seen, or the "surface" of the art, was given immanent value. This surface aesthetic came out of a code that was concerned only with technical skill and individual originality. Thus, Berger (1982) argues, rather than the visible being treated as signs addressed to the living, appearances were reduced to a fragmentary aspect of individuals' lives. "Visual art," Berger writes, "was severed from the belief that it was in the very nature of appearances to be meaningful" (p. 115). Appearances reconnected to our deepest aspirations and concerns provide an existential mapping where both the creator and the perceiver struggle to give meaning to their lives.

Art often presents us with issues of death and life. The distinction is an important one. The way of making sense of one's life can be attached to human temporality at either end, either birth or death. Hannah Arendt chose natality, or birth (as opposed to Heidegger's concern for mortality), which was connected to her concern for political action. She states (in Young-Bruehl, 1982), "Initiation of something new, action, is the human possibility that offers a glimmer of hope in political situations that could so easily become complete despair" (p. 495). Here, then, aesthetic practice connects to life understood in its dual formulation: it addresses itself to both the quest for human meaning and the struggle for human possibility in a world that frequently forecloses difference and imagination. The aesthetic is at once both existential and political. It overcomes the bifurcation of liberal ideology where each are seen as separate and isolated activities.

The possibility of the presence of new beginnings is perhaps where we can best understand that Art recognizes the significance of the human capacity to imagine and create—to liberate us from our own constructions.

Art must remain on the fringes of society to retain its liberating powers. Yet artists must not go too far from the real if their work is to reveal and indict reality, to hold within it the hope for change. Art must incorporate Freire's definition of authentic liberation as a praxis where one is engaged in reflection and action upon the world in order to transform it. Women as artists, must look at their own hopes and desires, coming together in the struggle to reshape all our lives. "Like it or not," writes Richard Morales (1990), "we [artists] are a part of a society's process of dreaming, thinking, and speaking to itself, reflecting our past, and finding new ways forward. Our greatest challenge is to accept that what we do with our work and with our lives is exactly as important as we believe our people and their world to be" (p. 24).

References

Adair, C. (1992). *Women and dance*. London: MacMillian.

Arvon. H. (1973). *Marxist esthetics*. London: Cornell University Press.

Benhabib, S., Butler, J., Cornell, D. & Fraser, N. (1995). *Feminist contentions*. New York: Routledge.

Berger, J. (1984). *And our faces, my heart, brief as photos*. New York: Pantheon Books.

Berger, J., & Mohr, J. (1982). *Another way of telling*. New York: Pantheon Books.

Cixous, H. (1980). The laugh of the medusa. In Elaine Marks & Isabelle de Courtivron (Eds.), *New French feminism: An anthology*. Massachusetts: University of Massachusetts Press.

Eagleton. T. (1996). *The illusions of postmodernism*. Oxford, UK: Blackwell.

Eagleton, T. (1990). *The ideology of the aesthetic*. Oxford, UK: Blackwell.

Estes, C. (1992). *Women who run with the wolves*. New York: Ballantine Books.

Fay, B. (1987). *Critical social science: Liberation and its limits.* New York: Cornell University Press.

Freire, P. (1988). *Pedagogy of the Oppressed.* New York: Continuum.

Gablik, S. (1984). *Has modernism failed?* New York: Thames and Hudson.

Hermann, C. (1980). Women in space and time. In Elaine Marks & Isabelle de Courtivron (Eds.), *New French feminism: An anthology.* Massachusetts: The University of Massachusetts Press.

Jameson, F. (1983). Postmodernism and consumer society. In Hal Foster (Ed.), *The anti-aesthetic.* Washington: Bay Press.

Kellner, D. (1984). *Herbert Marcuse and the crisis of marxism.* Los Angeles: University of California Press.

King, M. (1964). *Heidegger's philosophy.* New York: Macmillan.

Marcuse, H. (1969). *An essay on liberation.* Boston: Beacon Press.

Marcuse, H. (1978). *The Aesthetic Dimension.* Boston: Beacon Press.

Merleau-Ponty, M. (1994). *Phenomenology of perception.* London: Routledge.

Nicholson, L. (Ed.). (1990). *Feminism/Postmodernism.* New York: Routledge.

O'Brien, M., & Little, C. (Eds.). (1990). *Reimaging America: The arts for social change.* Philadelphia: New Society Publishers.

Sartre, J-P. (1957). *Existentialism and human emotion.* New Jersey: Citadel Press.

Stephanson, A. (1988). Regarding postmodernism: A conversation with Fredric Jameson. In A. Ross (Ed.), *Universal abandon,* (pp. 3-30). Minneapolis: University of Minnesota Press.

Welch, S. (1985). *Communities of resistance and solidarity.* New York: Orbis Books.

Wolff, J. (1981). *The social production of art.* New York: St. Martin's Press.

Young-Bruehl, E. (1982). *Hannah Arendt: For the love of the world.* London: Yale University Press.

CHAPTER SIX

Reaching beyond the Familiar: Redefining Dance Education as an Emancipatory Pedagogy

As Clarissa Pinkola Estes writes (1992), "we as woman must look to the killing thing that has gained hold of us, see the result of its grisly work, register it all consciously, and retain it in consciousness, and then act" (p. 58). The thing that has gained hold of us, of our female energy, is what Naomi Wolf (1991) names "the beauty myth." The tracks of it gouges, picks, marks, hides and embeds itself upon the flesh of our souls—the spirits of our bodies. It is an act of denigration of our fecund forms, our bushy eyebrows, flat-wide feet, nurturing flesh, musky smells, wise eyes, belly-deep voices and wide hip bones. We as women are to be captured in an image, forced into a relationship between that which isn't yet, and that which can never be. It is a place of nowhere and a state of no-being. How are we to find that slip of light revealing the forbidden door of knowing, of liberation? Where do we begin? We begin where all stories begin.

The Question of Meaning

For the past thirty years my life has been intimately defined by dance. I have studied dance, danced dances, made dances, watched dances, read about dance, taught dance, and shared many experiences with other dancers. The profession within which I work is called "dance education." What drew me to stay in the field for so many years becomes a question of meaning. By this I do not mean to say that dance "has given meaning" to my life. Rather, dance (as I have discovered) has been a place in society where I could remain on the margins, escape dull routinized work, be challenged to imagine and create, be reminded of myself as a whole person connecting mind and body, rechart my emotional life in time and space, and work through horizons of emotions and thoughts. Just the physical aspect of dancing alone provided a culturally acceptable avenue for me as a female to experience the erotic or full-of-life nature of dancing. Protected by art I could feel the full intensity of presence, but I could also disconnect from the world both past and future. I became, as Terry Eagleton (1980) has defined it, the ultimate liberal humanist: "radically depoliticized...free of enchainment to any...set of social beliefs which constitute us as subjects" (p. 99).

The very question of the meaning of freedom as a social condition where one is able to become subject of one's own identity and to participate in constructing the way one lives in the world is glossed over in the rhetoric of freedom, which is understood as an escape from the real conditions of our world. I argue that dance provides a vehicle for both the dancer and the audience to escape the material conditions of their lives—that is, dance is a preeminent symbol of freedom even if it is only an illusory freedom.

Examples of this relationship between dance and freedom abound. In popular culture for example, we see Tony Manero, in the film *Saturday Night Fever*, where he is able to transcend, at least psychologically, his working-class status every Saturday night at the disco. On the dance floor he becomes important and powerful, a leader of the group. Yet, in his everyday life, he is disempowered in his working-class status and ethnic identity, in an economic system that depends upon low-paying labor and devalues his cultural identity. In high culture, ballet presents us with an image of woman who is virginal, ethereal, childlike, transcending the material reality of her life represented by her pointe shoes and the man's lift. Ballroom dancing images the respectability of the petty bourgeois, i.e., providing a dance floor for fantasies out of another more romantic or elegant life. Broadway often represents another example of human life mimicking the escape from the real conditions of peoples' lives, to one of fantasy, glamour, and glitter. Even in such films as, *The*

Scent of a Woman, Al Pacino tangos as we revel at his control, gracefully commanding the space and his woman. In *Evita*, the tango is danced by groups of peasants as the passion of the poor; but in step, somberly, drained of energy, captured in space.

And, as for the professional dancer, almost every experience of dancing requires the dancer to transcend the everyday world. It surfaces palpably as she or he enters the dance space. The room is bare but for the barres and opposing mirrors. A few muffled voices greet others with recognition. The talk is of bodies. The air is left free for the voice of authority to speak the commands: "Let's begin." Surface images dominate the mind of the dancer— image and body. Space is made for the image, and with it the person as subject recedes. The body is left to the voice of authority—put into a mode of passivity as the dancer waits to be molded. Objectification of the body is a requirement. Its meaning and purpose becomes defined by its ability to re-present the correct image defined by the technical language of dance instruction. The dancer, knowing that she or he is valued and evaluated on surface appearance, learns to appraise her or himself in this way. The gaze of the external eye is internalized and the dancer sets up a double ego as both seer and the seen. Sandra Bartky (1990) refers to this as "narcissism."

The rites of passage in becoming a dancer most often reflects the same passage in becoming what is considered female in today's culture. The current female body fashion reflects the same cultural obsessions and preoccupations as with the dancer's body. Bartky defines the current body fashion:

> taut, small-breasted, narrow-hipped, and a slimness bordering on emaciation; it is a silhouette that seems more appropriate to an adolescent body or a newly pubescent girl than to an adult woman. (1990, p. 66)

Dieting and exercise becomes the necessary factors to obtain this image. Probably no one spends more time in front of a full-length mirror judging her appearance than a dancer. This preoccupation with the ideal physique is not a fad in dance. It is what being a dancer means. The following description is taken from a book concerning ballet *basics*:

> the female student longs to see the ideal reflection: a head neither too large nor too small, well-poised on a slim neck; shoulders of some width but with a slope gently downward; small bust, waist, buttocks; a back that is straight but not too rigid; well-formed arms hanging relaxed from the shoulders; delicate hands; slim, straight legs with smooth lines in the back and front; a compact foot that arches easily —all of this totaling a slim silhouette of ballet perfection. (Hammond, 1974, p. 104)

The author continues by defining the male image:

> The ideal male physique is not as specific, although it is generally considered to be strong, and well muscled without excess weight, or bulk, the shoulders wider than the waist and hips, and the height minimum of 5'6".

With this prescribed image of what a dancer is, the dancer's way of being in the world is circumscribed. The body, as sculpted object and highly-trained precision instrument, demands total attention. The technical language of ballet reinforces this prescribed image of the dancer. It emphasizes skills and training for proficiency, and therefore follows the scientific approach in its concern with dispassionate training and technical control. The student is valued for her or his ability to follow directions, replicate set skills, show commitment by virtually eliminating most other relationships and social roles, and by presenting an image of the dancer's body as little more than an automaton (vividly and depressingly described in Gelsey Kirkland's (1986) autobiography). In this approach the dancer learns to treat the body as object, an object submitted to rigorous training for the purpose of creating an image of perfection, an object mechanized for movement, and an object to be relinquished to authority, whether teacher, choreographer, or dance system. This is the dominant discourse of dance. Any other discourse is not considered to be "real" dance. Indeed, if we are not teaching technique classes in the college or university setting, then we must be teaching improvisational, compositional, or production skills. The discourse continues to be one that is inscribed by its skill orientation (See Shapiro 1995).

Living the Image
This kind of regulated existence rarely allows the dancer as subject to appear, much less develop. Living such a screened image subverts the possibility for giving meaning and purpose to one's life beyond dance. John Berger (1984) connects this disempowering effect to the dominant culture. "Every culture produces such a screen," writes Berger, "partly to facilitate its own practices and partly to consolidate its own powers" (pp. 72-73).

As artist-educators, we must ask ourselves whether we are complicit in creating such a screen, and if so, to whose powers do we relinquish our creativity and life energy, and whose purpose does it serve?

Carol Gilligan (1990) argues that "it is both psychologically and politically dangerous for girls not to know what is going on—or to render themselves innocent by disconnecting themselves from their bodies" (p. 523). She means here, of course, how females are conditioned to relate to their bodies. Being that dance classes are predominately attended by female students and dance is about the body, how can we not critically question our own traditions, which continue to oppress women? Replicated in the pedagogy of dance is what Paulo Freire refers to as the "banking concept" of education. In relation to the banking concept, dance classes are taught in a form that places the student in the position of doing what they are told, to accept a passive relationship to the teacher and the curriculum, and to separate dance knowledge and creative skills from other areas of their lives; in other words, when students come to dance class what they hear, talk, and learn about is dance in purely technical terms. We may teach modern, ballet, creative dance, and other forms of dance, but it is all bound in a language of technique, whether to ballet form or creative skills.

Despite the oppressive nature of dance, hundreds of little girls grow into womanhood and continue to find liberatory feelings in dancing. And if asked why they dance, the common response is, "Because it makes me feel good." This creates a peculiar paradox—feelings of liberation within an oppressive context. My own research (as seen in the previous chapter) into why women dance produced answers like these:

☞ *Dance is important because it gives you a sense of yourself....*
It gives you a way of finding your place in the world.

☞ *Dance is important because it has allowed me to do what I*
want to do...it gives me a vehicle to go beyond where I
thought it was possible to go.

Typically, I have found that women who are modern dancers speak about finding identity, place, and transformation. The experience of dance, as one in which the self is located in time and space, can appear to overcome the fragmentation and alienation so present in the modern world. Their descriptions speak to finding a place where women can experience control over their bodies, take up space, and be physically strong. In this way the modern dancer represents to us the struggles of many women today. She embodies clearly much that feminist and postmodern observers have noted in our culture about the body—as image, as object, as escape, and as possibility.

These young women do not question, however, the ever-present desire to become the ideal image or the fact that most dance classes are based on skill development and competition. They do not question a system that accepts and rejects one based on the appearance of the body. And they do not question the separation of the dancer's life from the dance experience. Rather, she (the dancer) senses the liberation of her body in an unconscious way, of taking control of her body, of taking up space, moving with strength and energy, exhibiting power, presenting herself consciously for the gaze of "other." She becomes freed to be in that time and space, in the ever-present now of dance; liberated from the everyday oppressions that she still does not name. It is an escape which precludes a critical understanding of what freedom as a woman might really mean. Her desire, expressed through the dance experience, is to feel alive; to be imaginative and creative; to work in a community intimately and in solidarity with others; to participate in creating and changing her image; and to express the silences, absences, and gaps from the "officially" constructed image of women. The body of the dancer makes manifest the desire for another way of being in the world. She embodies the hope for freedom even in her cliched, stereotyped roles from virginal ballerina to dance-hall queen. Yet, unable to connect her individual feelings to the social context from which they arise, the dancer is left in a state where there are no real-life existential openings or choices.

Unlike the image of the ballerina, the modern dancer's body displays the search for another identity; for a place other than one that rejects the fullness of her being; for work that is rooted in creativity and community, and that remembers the powers of the sensual along with the intellectual. I believe that in this there is hope. This hope is rooted in an awareness of incompleteness that moves the dancer into an existential search. It is a search for authentic existence through the liberation of the body—but one, unfortunately, in which the dancer falls short. Freire (1988) defines "authentic liberation" as one that calls for action and reflection of women and men upon their world in order to transform it. The key distinction here reminds us that personal transformation can never be separated from changing the world in which we live. Authentic liberation, as Freire has argued, must first start from our recognition of how *we are situated in relation to the world, rather than separate from it.* Authentic existence—that which many artists believe they are struggling for—becomes mutilated without the possibility for liberation from the concrete conditions of our existence. This kind of *education for self and social transformation* is mostly absent in the field of dance education.

Tangled Theories or Subverting the Tango

My own struggle to connect dance pedagogy to liberation has lead me through tangled histories from Marx to Imelda Marcos. I have linked the choice of economic systems to the kind of shoes women wear. More succinctly, I have pioneered a critical pedagogy of the body in dance while teaching at a small, private liberal-arts college for women (therefore, in my further writing in this chapter, I will be referring only to women's experiences). Subverting the traditional pedagogic formulas for dance, I have been able to re-flesh the dancer to an embodied existence through a choreographic process that makes connections between feminist work and a liberatory pedagogy. My intention in all of this is to connect women with a pedagogy which emphasizes their life experience and values their voices; one that has as its purpose the empowerment of women by means of gaining critical understanding of the self in relationship to society, and by understanding their bodies, not as objects of hostility, but as something that is to be valued, indeed cherished.

The body uses its skin, flesh, and spirit to record all that goes on around it. It carries a living record, as Estes (1992) writes, of

> life given, life taken, life hoped for and life healed. It is valued for its articulate ability to register immediate reaction, to feel profoundly, to sense ahead.... It speaks through the leaping of the heart, the falling of the spirit, the pit at the center, and rising hope.... Like a sponge filled with water, anywhere the flesh is pressed, wrung, even touched lightly, a memory may flow out in a stream. (p. 200)

To understand the knowledge of the body in this sense is antagonistic to the dominant traditions in dance situated in a society that attempts to circumscribe women's ways of knowing by objectifying the body, carving it up and starving it out, and creating fractures and fissures that in turn fragment women's identity and power.

"EATING: Dying to be Thin" (the title of a dance) is an example of how creating a dance can be a dialectical process that engages the students in an understanding of the self as an embodied domain of a culture's values, contentions, and compliances. Specifically, the dancers were involved in reflecting upon their relationship to food and how this leads to self-deprivation, destroying female autonomy and eroding self-esteem. Naomi Wolf (1991) contends that the issue is not simply one of food, but extends beyond, "making women feel poor and think poor...she is weak, sexless and voiceless, and can only with difficulty focus on a world beyond her plate" (p. 197). With my students, we critically examined how these issues affect how we feel about, live in, and live with our own bodies. We noted that, as women, it is in our bodies that we primarily experience who we are, and it is in our bodies that we struggle with issues of self-acceptance, affirmation, social action, and how we relate to other women. Simply stated, we were in a process of re-membering our bodies.

Because the dance was about the lives of dancers who were predominately white, Southern middle-class women, their stories reflect this. Rather than experiencing this as an obstacle, we address the particularities of their situation and also its connections to the broader content of women's lives. Following is a description of the choreographic/pedagogic process.

The first part of the dance, "Forbidden Fruit," ties into the construction of femininity where, in a society that has an abundance of food, one is engaged in a hunger strike, compulsively suppressing hunger as a response to a female image that is fleshless, indeed "wiggleless." The process began with a reflection. I asked the dancers to think about rituals they have developed around food. This is where the table appeared in the dance, symbolizing the ever-present issue of eating. We talked about how our responses to food and eating have become mechanical: taking only half a piece of bread, carefully placing chosen amounts of food on our plates, always knowing the number of fat grams (the most recent index of women's oppression). I ask the dancers to reflect upon the first time they could remember becoming aware of weight. They recalled an understanding of what normal size was suppose to be and how that image was fixed and corresponded to the Barbie image, already creating a contradictory message of thin but "with breasts." The words they chose to represent their thoughts in movement were "scary," "worried," and "obsessive."

The depletion of time and energy as a result of the obsession with hunger and thinness became apparent for the first time. There began to be an understanding that through this control axis, that is, between starvation and perfection, there is an usurping of women's energy as it is directed toward the mastery of the body. Their mastery of body weight was clearly tied to a sense of moral virtue. Those who cannot sustain the battle with food present an image that is viewed by the culture representing a lack of self-management and self-determination. Indeed, we name and perceive of them as slobs, lazy, unreliable, uncaring, lower class, and even stupid. They lack will and, therefore, are morally and personally inadequate. Yet, fat is sexual in women. Fat tissues store sex hormones, so low fat reserves are linked to low levels of estrogen and other important sex hormones. That is why it isn't uncommon to hear of women who zealously exercise having menstrual irregularities and diminished fertility.

Today the body of the model is 22 to 23 percent leaner than that of an average woman (Bordo, 1994). Thinness representing upward mobility—"You can never be too thin or too rich"— opens the way for an exploitative marketing strategy presenting instant gratification: "From Fat to Fabulous in 21 Days," "Size 22 to Size 10 in No Time Flat," "Six Minutes to an Olympic Class Stomach," "3,000 Sit-Ups without moving an inch," "Ten Miles of Jogging Lying Flat on Your Back," and then, of course, the instant technological miracle of liposuction promising to suck out extra fat. We are continually being taught to see the body as our enemy; eating as war.

As part of creating the dance, we watched the film *Eating,* where, at a birthday party, a piece of cake is passed around a large circle of women and it returns to the front not taken. We discussed the social pressure placed upon women centered on eating, and how eating permeates all other aspects of our lives. Eating turns into a life-threatening issue. For example, The Diet Centers' diet is fixed at daily 1,600 calories; in the Lodz Ghetto in 1941, Jews were allotted starvation rations of 500-1,220 calories a day! At the Treblinka concentration camp, 900 calories was determined to be the daily minimum necessary to sustain human functioning. Today, Wolf reminds us, at the nation's top weight-loss clinics the rations are the same. With constant semistarvation there is a coarsening of emotions and sensitivity to others. Symptoms such as irritability, listlessness, apathy, poor concentration, fatigue, anxiety, depression, and social isolation accompany the state of semi-starvation. Hunger drives the person to be antisocial and obsessive about food.

I brought into the rehearsal a gallon of Breyers' ice cream with cups and spoons for everyone and said, "Here, please eat." The dancers responded with glee and a sense of celebration and then quickly stated, "I can't eat any"; "Tomorrow it would show up in my leotard"; and "I will eat a little" (taking only a couple of spoonfuls.) We talked about their response to the ice cream. Words that expressed their reactions to this loss of pleasure became the basis for the second section of the dance named *The Famine Within*. This section creates external images of the internal struggles.

They read the chapter "Hunger" from *The Beauty Myth* (Wolf, 1991) and shared the horror from realizing the extent to which women have embodied self-hate and self-abnegation of their bodies—and themselves. They realized their own political disempowerment and self-denial through the loss of life energy. The documentary, "The Famine Within," which correlates mass media's image of the beautiful woman and the rise of anorexia and bulimia in today's culture of young women, brought to the fore that it is no longer a private issue. About 60 to 80 percent of college women deny themselves adequate nutrition; of dancers, 38 percent show anorexic behavior. The average model, dancer, or actress, claims Wolf, is thinner than 95 percent of the female population. Their ultimate goal is to reach a point where they don't have to eat at all. *They are dying to be thin.*

Our group went to a high school to work with a dance class of female students. We engaged these students in reflective writings around issues of body image and eating. Driving back to Meredith College in the van, I ask the dancers to imagine what it would be like not to have these kinds of relationships to eating and food. They responded with elation—"wonderful," "freed energy," "lifted burden," and a recognition of the need for women to support other women. In the final section of the dance, the dancers attempt to re-create the eating table and struggle to re-experience food as a blessing. And, for the first time in the dance, they see each other, physically touch each other, and encompass a spirit of resistance with their arms around each other's waists forming a circle. Speaking through the voices of their bodies in motion, they put before the audience the question of consciousness—where are you in this dance of life?

A Different Language for Movement

By listening to the language of our own teaching we find the gaping absence of a discourse that might make it possible for students to question why they dance, what body experiences they have when dancing, and how they might make sense of them in relation to their everyday body experiences; such classes can encourage them to critically reflect upon who they are, and how that is influenced by the larger culture in which they live. Such a pedagogy might make apparent that our bodies mirror the culture from which we come (Shapiro, 1996, 1998). Without critically questioning the re-creation of dance experiences and the dancer's image, we risk perpetuating the objectification of the female body and the "official" language which binds it. There is then a vital need for us as dance educators to confront our particular views of dance education, shifting our paradigm for conceptualizing dance to one that recognizes the value of a pedagogic process that engages the individual to reflect upon, gain understanding of, and give meaning to one's life. The separations between art and life, dancer and world, and individual and society need to be overcome. Dance must be connected to the world in order to re-create and re-shape the world. We must speak a new language, one that cries out against a trivialized notion of arts and aesthetic experiences, and against the oppression of women. We must insist that dance education focuses upon what it means to be a woman and a human being, and how aesthetic experiences make possible the ability to re-image what the world ought to be. It must connect our care, love, and concerns as human beings to a pedagogy for dance that seeks to create a space for healing, repairing, and transformation of the world—one where there is a strong moral commitment to human liberation and social justice. The implications for dance are nothing short of revolutionary. What we must do is re-envisage dance in terms of a critical pedagogy where the body/subject can give voice and expression to everyday life with all of its indignities, injustices, and oppressive silences. Such a pedagogy can then reconnect dance to the struggle for a freer and more caring world. With few exceptions, dance education has not yet begun to take seriously this responsibility.

References

Adair, C. (1992). *Women and dance*. London: MacMillian.

Adorno, T., & Horkheimer, M. (1972). *Dialectic of enlightenment*. (J. Cumming, Trans.). New York: Herder & Herder.

Bartky, S. (1990). *Femininity and domination*. New York: Routledge.

Benjamin, W. (1969). *Illuminations*. London: Schocken.

Berger, J. (1984). *And our faces, my heart, brief as photos*. New York: Pantheon Books.

Berger, J. (1980). *About looking*. New York: Pantheon Books.

Berman, M. (1989). *Coming to our senses*. New York: Simon and Schuster.

Bordo, S. (1994). *Unbearable weight*. Berkeley: University of California Press.

Boyce, J., Daly, A., Jones, B.T., & Martin, C. (1988). Movement and gender. *TDR*, 32(4), 82- 101.

Brumberg, J. (1988). *Fasting girls*. Cambridge: Harvard Press.

Carter, S. (1991, January). Children of crisis. *Z Magazine*, 33-35.

Eagleton, T. (1990). *The ideology of the aesthetic*. Cambridge: Basil Blackwell.

Eagleton, T. (1980). The subject of literature. *Cultural Critique*, 3, 95-104.

Estes, C. (1992). *Women who run with the wolves*. New York: Ballantine Books.

Freire, P. (1988). *Pedagogy of the oppressed*. New York: Continuum Publishing Company.

Gilligan, Carol. (1990, Winter). Joining the resistance: Psychology, politics, girls and women. The female body, *Michigan Quarterly Review*, XXIX (4), 501-536.

Goldstein, L. (Ed.). (1991). *The female body*. Michigan: University of Michigan Press.

Greene, M. (1991). Texts and margins. *Harvard Educational Review*, 1(61), 27-38.

Greene, M. (1988). *The dialectic of freedom*. New York: Teachers College Press.

Grigsby, D. (1990, Winter). Dilemmas of visibility: Contemporary women artists' representations of female bodies. The female body, *Michigan Quarterly Review*, XXIX(4), 584-601.

Hammond, S. (1974). *Ballet basics*. California: Maryfield Publishing.

Jacobus, M., Keller, E. & Shuttleworth, S. (1990). *Body/politics*. New York: Routledge.

Kirkland, G. (1986). *Dancing on my grave*. New York: Doubleday.

Langeveld, M. (1984). How does the child experience the world of things. *Phenomenology & Pedagogy*, 2(3), 215-223.

McLaren, P. (1989). *Life in schools*. New York: Longman Press.

Middleton, S. (1993). *Educating feminists*. New York: Teachers College Press.

Nicholson, L. (1990). *Feminism/postmodernism*. New York: Routledge.

Novack, C. (1988). Looking at movement as culture. *TDR, 32*(4), 102-119.

Shapiro, S. (1998). Dance, power, and difference: Critical and feminist perspectives on dance education. Illinois: Human Kinetics.

Shapiro, S. (1996). Towards transformative teachers: Critical and feminist perspectives on dance education. *Impulse,* (1), 37-48.

Shapiro, S. (1995). Studies in dancer's lives: Feminist and post-modern perspectives. *Research Quarterly for Exercise and Sport Abstracts Supplement.*

Sklar, H. (1990, November). American dreams, American nightmares. *Z Magazine*, 41-44.

Stinson, S. (1988). *Dance for young children.* Virginia: American Alliance for Health, Physical Education, Recreation, and Dance.

Taylor, (Shapiro) S. (1991). Skinned alive: Towards a postmodern pedagogy of the body. *Education Society*, 9(1), 61-72.

Taylor, (Shapiro) S. (1990). Stripping images; or what am I doing up here taking my clothes off? *Dance and the female body in critical pedagogy.* Unpublished presentation of dance performance and research interview for JCT Conference.

Taylor, (Shapiro) S. (1989). *The existential dimension of the dancer's life.* Unpublished research paper.

Wolf, N. (1991). *The beauty myth.* New York: William Morrow and Company, Incorporated.

CHAPTER SEVEN

Towards a Critical Pedagogy of the Body

The emergence of the body as a focus for the study of culture, power, and resistance is demonstrated in the abundant writing on the subject currently in circulation. It is apparent that much of what has been said is more in the way of a metareflection on the importance of recognizing the nature of the postmodern body; understanding how it is inscribed by culture, mediates power, and expresses resistance to the normalizing practices of the society. What is rarely found in such work is a pedagogy where the body/subject as a lived medium becomes part of the curriculum. It is precisely this concern that is central to this book and addressed in this chapter.

Here, the attempt is to look at the theoretical and practical implications for a critical pedagogy of the body in a postmodernist discourse. I draw on recent work found in the fields of feminist and postmodern scholarship, critical studies of education, and recent developments in dance and gender. Central to this, for me, has been rethinking the Western philosophic tradition in regard to the Cartesian duality of mind and body. In this, the body is seen as the site of epistemological limitation—which must be overcome if one is to understand things as they really are, undistorted by human experience or perspective. Such a view is foundational to the whole positivist educational enterprise with its notion of knowledge unsullied by human passions, feelings, and emotions; that is, by the presence of the body. It is against this excision of the human body from the process of knowing that so much postmodern and feminist scholarship has been aimed, and more particularly, where my work is situated. Later in this chap-

ter I will describe, in some detail, a curriculum project that is
guided by a philosophy of critical pedagogy that makes the
body/subject the focus of education. The curriculum is one that
explores, through the modality of modern dance, the way in which
women's voices, and therefore choices, are circumscribed by the
culture. Providing this description is important in order to give
some real sense of what a critical pedagogy of the body might
look like. I also want to note here my belief (and I will return to
this in the conclusion) that much of postmodern thinking about
the body is still caught in a language that is objectifying, and in so
doing, denies the possibilities of human agency. Nonetheless, as I
make clear below, its importance to my own intellectual and practical development should not be underestimated.

For those of us who have struggled to develop liberational
pedagogies, the advent of postmodern ideas, concepts, and theories have presented an important challenge to our work. They
have questioned our confidence about the legitimacy of the
methodological dimensions, as well as the possible outcomes, of
our teaching (Giroux, 1992). Postmodernism, for example, has
demonstrated the questionable basis of our emancipatory inten-
tions. The hitherto transcendent moral referents of critical pedagogy—freedom, justice, and autonomy—have become aspects of
the *grand recits*—the metanarratives—of a very particular historical and cultural period (Welch, 1985). Their universal impera-
tives have contained the seeds of new discursive regimes of
power and authority (Lyotard, 1984; Foucault, 1980). No longer
to be seen as an end of power, transformational politics or pedagogy must inevitably contain the seeds of new regimes of
"power/knowledge" (Welch, 1985). Such notions have confronted critical teachers with the difficult recognition of the thin line
that separates attempts to "free" students from our complicity in
imposing on them new, perhaps more subtle, forms of domination (Ellsworth, 1989). In this respect we are all now the children
of Foucault, seeing the social world as forever bound in webs of
authority and power. Of course, to lose our innocence about the
ubiquity of power even in the most liberational of classrooms is
to undercut our convictions, potentially at least, about the possi-

bility of genuinely democratic educational spaces (Burbules & Rice, 1991). We have also to view our own role as teachers with much more wary eyes. This has certainly been apparent in the important interventions in critical pedagogy by certain feminist writers who have pointed to the hidden uses of power even by those committed to a transformational education (Luke & Gore 1992). Critical pedagogues arrogate to themselves the superior capacity to decode the experience and meanings of students—a practice that in this account must inevitably reconstruct the hierarchical structures of schools.

All of this presents complex challenges to radical teachers. Can we fully accept the inevitably asymmetrical distribution of power in our classrooms and take seriously the goal of student empowerment? The task, we have come to see, is much more difficult than we had assumed. It is easy to see how some have concluded that we must abandon all attempts to demystify the false or distorted understandings of our students, replacing this with classrooms that provide opportunities for the sharing of essentially incommensurable narratives. As understandable as this position is, I believe it represents an abandonment of a radical democratic project that must confront the reality of powerful mass media (Kellner, 1988). These certainly do seek to create ways of seeing and knowing that distort and deflect us from grasping the circumstances that shape our own lives. This embrace of narrative, and reluctance to critique the ideology, points to postmodern's erosion of an ontological referent (Eagleton, 1991). Talk of a "really-existing reality" has been eliminated by deconstructive critique that refuses a "metaphysics of presence" (West, 1989). Where before critical social analysis could point confidently to the distinctions between surface and substructure, now it is asserted there is only the semiotic play that constitutes surfaces (Baudrillard, 1983, 1981). It is not only positivistic notions of truth that are dethroned by such claims, so is the whole tradition of emancipatory praxis that rested on the grounds of some accurate human grasp of reality (Smart, 1992). Where "reality" is only one possible narrative among many possibilities, on what basis can we act? (Svi Shapiro, 1991). Indeed under the influence of this Nietzschian view we have been forced to face the full consequences of a world where our ethical and political commitments have been brutally cut loose from all claims, to be anchored in some Archimedean point of knowing (Kariel, 1989). If one discourse or language is given more value than another, this is not because of its intrinsic character or "truth," but because of the way this version of reality organizes our perceptions and understandings of the world. And every such version of reality is tied in with the exercise of power by one group or another. There is no ultimate reference point for truth outside of a history that might make it become true. In a world where brutalities, injustice, and degradation demand resolute and determined human response there is the paradox of increasing uncertainty about what we know, and the ethical and political commitments that are consequences of this knowledge.

It is clear that postmodern notions have offered a series of important challenges to our ideas about a critical or liberational pedagogy. They have also opened up important considerations. Not the least of these concerns the decentering of authority, and an attention to peripheral voices, texts, languages, and experiences. Identity has been radically freed from essentialist, prejudicial or regionally-fixed constructions. Svi Shapiro (in press) states:

> Identity is now often viewed as a tyranny that seeks to 'fix' us in a particular mode or affect—the result of a specific play of power and knowledge.... Indeed freedom from this point of view becomes our ability to explode the apparent obviousness of any given identity and show how it is entirely a figment of a suppressed relational cultural grid. Black is the obverse of white; female of male; Jew of Christian and so on.... Such thinking, I need hardly add, has powerfully upset those dangerous, racist, misogynist or homophobic categories that paint human beings into permanent and enclosed social spaces.

It must be added, however, that the effects that have denaturalized and de-essentialized cultural and gendered identities have also left us with little to affirm. They appear to have swept away the grounds for memory and historically-constituted identities without which political agency and ethical commitment seem hard to imagine. Yet, one cannot ignore the immense importance of postmodern theory in its recognition of the place and construction of the "other" in the culture, and its role in the constitution of the socially normative (Giroux & McLaren, 1994). Nor can we overlook the challenge to long-accepted views of subjectivity and the self—one that dethrones the rational and autonomous ego. Perhaps, however, the most intriguing of the consequences of postmodern thought concerns the body, out of which has developed what Peter McLaren has called the "pedagogy of enfleshment" (McLaren, 1988). And this is the concern in the remainder of this chapter.

The Specific, the Local, and the Body

A number of writers have noted that the emergence of the body in postmodern intellectual and pedagogic work is rooted in a reappraisal of the Western philosophic tradition—especially in regard to the Cartesian duality of mind and body (Nicholson, 1990). Susan Bordo has noted that in Cartesian epistemology the body is conceptualized as the site of epistemological limitation, which fixes the knower in time and space, and thereby situates and relativizes perception and thought (Bordo, 1993). It is the body that must be overcome—that must be transcended—if one is to achieve the "view from nowhere" or the "God's-eye view" through which one can see things as they really are, undistorted by human experience or perspective. Of course such a view is foundational to the whole positivist research enterprise with its notion of knowledge unclouded by human passions, feelings, emotions, etc.; that is, intellection unsullied by the presence of the body. Of course, it is possible to see in this not only the Cartesian view of mind separated from body, but also the influence of Augustinian Christianity with its disdain for the flesh, and the bourgeois masculinist desire to distance and control nature (Eagleton, 1990). And it is against this attempted excision of the human body from the process of knowing that so much postmodern and feminist scholarship has been aimed. Feminists, for example, have connected the quest for universal reason to the privileging of human experience disconnected from time or space (Harding, 1990). Postmodern critique, especially in its deconstructionist form, has opposed the ideal of disembodied knowledge, which it sees as an impossibility and a mystification. In fact there is no escape from human presence and position in the world. From this perspective there is no escape from the body. Indeed, the body, far from being an obstacle to knowing, "is seen instead as the vehicle of the human making and remaking of the world, constantly shifting location, capable of revealing endlessly new points of view" (Bordo, 1993). This affirmation of the body as integral to the process of knowing opens up a whole new terrain for epistemological inquiry. We can begin to talk of sentient knowledge as opposed to the disembodied reason for so long venerated by Western philosophical tradition.

This turn to the body in both feminist and postmodern writing is part of the broader epistemological and political shift towards the specific, the contingent, and the local (Hutcheon, 1989; Rosenau, 1992). It is tied in with the disillusionment and, for some, abandonment of universal assertions and models (Harvey, 1989). In whatever form such universal claims appear-Marxism, science or social science, liberalism—they are seen as always marginalizing or excluding difference, and normalizing the center over what is at the periphery. Thus such theorizing instantiates the West's culture and development over other parts of the globe; it relegates homosexuality to the realm of the "unnatural"; trivializes, or disparages women's experience. The search for what is universal is deeply embedded in the intellectual psyche of the Western philosophical tradition. Its consequence is the elevation of discourses that speak to what is typical, what is standard, and what normal (Bauman, 1991). Whether it admits to it or not, Western philosophical tradition seeks knowledge and understanding that seems to transcend place and time. Of course in this context the body represents an entirely antithetical language. It is one of place, temporality, particularity, and ineffability. For those who seek to write from the body, the flesh becomes, both substantively and metaphorically, a place of engagement with a life's pain, aches, desires, and ecstasies (Berger, 1984;

hooks, 1990). It is a knowledge that is never fully recoverable so that there can be no illusions about the veracity of our discourse. Yet nor can there be any doubt about its power to evoke and to resonate with all that is most gut-wrenching and visceral in our existence. It is the return of an aesthetic language that is no more the marginal or fantastical stepchild of modernity, but one that takes us to the heart of being itself, to what Marx referred to as "species"—life itself.

The emphasis on the specific, the local, and the body has been, of course, enormously influenced by the work of Michel Foucault. Foucault shifted the analysis and understanding of power from Marx's preponderantly single axis of domination to a highly complex, dispersed notion of power—one that runs through institutions, social practices, forms of knowledge, and through the body itself in highly specific and differentiated ways. In this sense dominance is not sustained or imposed from above, but through a multiplicity of "processes of different origin and scattered location" (Bordo, 1993). In doing, so she continues, "it regulates the most intimate and minute elements of the construction of space, time, desire, and embodiment" (p. 27). Bordo summarizes the importance of Foucault's analysis.

> For Foucault, modern (as opposed to sovereign) power is non-authoritarian, non-conspiratorial, and indeed non-orchestrated; yet it nonetheless produces and normalizes bodies to serve prevailing relations of dominance and subordination. Understanding this new sort of power requires, according to Foucault, two conceptual changes. First, we must cease to imagine power as the *possession* of individuals or groups—as something people "have"—and instead see it as a dynamic of non-centralized forces. Second, we must recognize that these forces are *not* random or haphazard, but configure to assume particular historical forms, within which certain groups and ideologies *do* have dominance. (p. 26)

Bordo (p. 28) notes that this Foucauldian view is extraordinarily helpful to a feminist analysis of the contemporary "normalizing" discipline of diet and exercise, and to an understanding of eating disorders, "practices which train the female body in docility and

obedience to cultural demands while at the same time being
experienced in terms of power and control." She notes, however,
that in Foucault's later writings he emphasized that power relations are "never seamless." They are always producing new
forms of culture and subjectivity, and new opportunities for resistance and transformation:

> Where there is power, he came to see, there is also resistance.
> Dominant forms and institutions are continually being penetrated and
> reconstructed by values, styles, and know ledges that have been
> developing and gathering strength, energy, and distinctiveness "at the
> margins".... Such transformations do not occur in one fell swoop; they
> emerge only gradually, through local and often minute shifts in power.
> They may also be served, paradoxically, through conformity to pre-
> vailing norms. So, for example, the woman who goes into a rigorous
> weight-training program in order to achieve the currently stylish look
> may discover that her new muscles give her the self-confidence that
> enables her to assert herself more forcefully at work. Modern power-
> relations are thus unstable; resistance is perpetual and hegemony pre-
> carious. (pp. 27-28)

This instability of modern power relations, as possibilities for
either embodied repression or liberation, reveals the incompati-
bility of any theory that decenters the subject to the point of elim-
ination. Clearly, only a relatively coherent self can consider
notions of self or social transformation. This is the starting point
of my project in critical pedagogy; that is, a philosophy of praxis concerned with emancipation, and committed to a process that
connects self-reflection and understanding to a knowledge that
makes transformation of the social conditions we live possible. It
begins by making it possible for the silenced experiences of students to speak in the classroom about their own concerns, desires,
and needs. It remakes the curriculum into a dialectic between
their particular hermeneutic of the lived world and the explanatory narrative of a critical theoretical framework. My own chore-
ographic/pedagogic process reflects these concerns. The example
discussed below is explained in great detail in the hopes of clarifying ways in which pedagogic practices can involve the
body/subject in helping students to develop a critical understand-

ing of their world in terms of issues of power and control. The project described here is part of an ongoing educational project developed over several years and it emphasizes the importance of the affective and the sensual as modes of understanding our lives and our world. This approach challenges the dominance of a tradition that has been exclusively focused on rational and intellectual forms of knowing. This process, which I call a "critical choreographic/pedagogic project," is based in my work as a dance educator at a small, southern, private liberal-arts college for women. From their own stories, the women dancers who participated in the project created movements that allowed them to re-present images, through dance, that express the deeply inscribed nature of female identity in our culture. Through readings, reflections, viewing of documentaries and movies, and discussions, we elicited "body memories," which became the source for dance movements. These memories are constructed out of the discourses and the culture in which students live, and they provide a depth and emotional richness that allowed students to become profoundly aware of their struggles for identity and agency. From this process of articulation and embodied expression, they were able to better understand and grapple with the possibilities for confronting and transforming the way they live their lives. In all of this, the body is conceived as the interface of the individual and society; as the "terrain of flesh" where ideological structures are inscribed; as the material base that holds knowledge; as that which can "tell the stories" of the lives we live. Though the field of dance, like no other art form, deals directly with the body, dance, as an art form, in fact, has an obsessive focus on matters of technique and performance, and as far as females are concerned is, arguably, a highly repressive aesthetic practice (S. Shapiro & S. Shapiro, 1995). Dance education, while having some tradition of self-expression, is rooted for the most part in that bourgeois artistic vision of the free self that is able to transcend material existence and occupy a "higher realm" of spiritual values and existence (Eagleton, 1985). There is, typically, little here that connects dance education to a critical apprehension of culture or a socially-constructed subjectivity.

It is precisely this that impels the curricular exercise titled "Silent Voices" described in the next section. In its participatory choreographic process, the use of dialogue, as well as in its clearly political concerns, this is a form of dance education that runs against the grain, violating some of the more sacred tenets of modern dance and modern dance instruction. The process, I might add, has been an emotionally and cognitively profound one, frequently affecting students in transformative ways. It becomes clear that the body, or more precisely, the body/subject, is a powerful focus for an emancipatory pedagogy. The pedagogic work described is narrated in the first person. This, it is hoped, captures some of the intensity, vitality, and emotional resonance of the educational project. The descriptive portions in the section below are meant to convey a sense of the images and movements in the dance. Quite obviously these movements are meant to be seen and experienced visually.

Silent Voices:
Dance Education and the Process of Liberation

> Silence a position in which women experience themselves as mindless and voiceless and subject to the whims of external authority. (Belenky, Clinchy, Goldberger & Tarule, *Women's Ways of Knowing,* 1986 p. 15)

The choreographic/pedagogic process I will be describing has taken place within the college setting with rehearsals regularly scheduled during the semester, meeting twice a week for one and one-half hours. The exception to this is during the week of performance when we meet in the theatre each evening for the marking of stage space, creating lighting designs, checking sound levels and ending with dress rehearsal.

Dancers who are involved in the project are chosen at the beginning of the fall semester from those who are in the performing dance theatre of the college (this is only because it is a departmental rule). Purposefully, I select with an awareness of those dancers who are interested in the field of dance education, or that I have experienced as being open to reflection and moving beyond their "taken-for-granted" state. I begin the process with an issue that appears to be resonant with felt experiences, as well as, potentially transformative to their subjectivity.

"Silent Voices," as a title, already references the complexity of the notion that voices can be silenced, silent, or unheard. It was in these three ways that the pedagogy was directed—how women are silenced, when women choose to remain silent, and how silencing occurs when one speaks but is not heard. From my own experience teaching at a private southern liberal-arts college for women (and growing up as a southern woman myself), I came to an understanding of the debilitating effects of Southern culture on women's voices. To be a woman and to be Southern represents a double bind. For in southern culture, "girls" embody those pleasant, polite, and unopinionated characteristics that make it impossible to question, to express a viewpoint other than the accepted, or to be in conflict of any sort. To speak out, question, or debate places one in a category of being a "northerner," which means to be aggressive, loud, and vulgar: a troublemaker. The act of speaking for a young woman is not a simple one. This action places her in the space of moral judgement. She knows she will be labeled one way or another.

Influenced by feminist and critical pedagogy, my teaching is directed toward "giving voice" to students. Yet, I have found the notion of "giving" to be problematic in itself. I can ask questions and provide the students both the space and time to speak and I can listen and try to hear what their concerns are. But I cannot "give" them their voice. They must do that for themselves. And that has become my struggle: How do we come to name our own forms of oppression and liberation?

And so we began. The broad issue given to the dancers was how are women silenced—*how have you been silenced?* I broke this down into the three separate questions referred to earlier. Throughout the process the dancers engaged these questions by reflecting on, connecting to, and naming their own experiences. In our first meeting, I asked each student to write something important for us to know about them on an index card. When they had completed these, each dancer was instructed to read her card without interruption while the rest of us would do anything but listen. Each dancer completed the process. After the experience I began a dialogue based on how it felt to not be heard when sharing something important about oneself. Words gave significance to the experience: "frustrated," "hurt," "angry," "lonely," "unimportant," "alienated"; and words that described their reactions to these situations: "isolating," "giving up," "losing purpose," "withdrawing." Mixed in with the descriptions of the immediate experience were memories of previous ones: "This is just like when I tell my father I want to be a teacher more than anything else, but he doesn't hear me"; and "Yeah, I was talking the other day while there was a bunch of guys watching the game and it was as if I wasn't even there"; and "I wanted to get up and walk out when the professor looked at me and asked, Ms. Williams, can you answer the question? He didn't want to hear what I thought, he just wanted the correct answer—his answer—to the question." The first section of the dance was developed from out of these discussions. I listed their words in two sections on the board, one section from their felt experiences and the other from how they responded to those experiences, and then asked each dancer to choose three words from each. Next, they were asked to express those words in movement—uniting here thought, feeling, and movement or action. From their individual movement sequences we created the first section of the dance. Each dancer taught their sequences to the others, and I, as choreographer, placed them into ordered patterns. As they worked, other memories began to surface and were spoken. And as they re-experienced their tacit knowing while developing their movement sequences, their level of anger increased. The bond between them grew with the recognition of their shared suffering as their bodies "remembered" the indignities and the pain.

> The dance begins on the floor, all women on their knees, hands covering their faces, moving back and forth in a sobbing fashion. They release into the floor knees pulled against stomachs as they roll on their backs side to side. Ending face down against the floor, they push

their heavy bodies with their arms, and slide backwards. Turning onto their sides, diagonally in a fetal position, they begin to draw a continuous figure eight with their fingertips. Slowly, they drag their torsos to a sitting position, continuing to physically mark their spaces and that inscribe their bodies—this time with the sensed boundaries. Rising to full standing as if moving through heavy liquid, they grab their hair, pulling it upwards toward the ceiling, and then, collapse with a heave—arms and heads left hanging limply from their bent positions. They repeat this hair pulling and collapse. Stillness. As if from inside their bodies, small movements initiate a shaking and jerking until the disturbances are so large the dancers are forced to move out of place.

While I have chosen the larger issue (in this case, how white, southern middle-class women are silenced in today's society), the direction of our discussions come from the telling of the dancers' stories—from the experiences of their own lives. It is the dancers who give a narrative concreteness to the abstracted question. For example, what is made clear in our dialogue is that almost all situations in which they had felt silenced were ones involving men, whether father, friend, professor, or dating companion. Other women were unanimously named as preferred companions in regard to discussing personal matters. (Silencing by other women arose in our later discussions and centered around competition.)

As our time together passed, their reflective questioning deepened and encompassed father-mother-daughter relationships—analyzing especially the role of their mothers in relationship to their fathers. They discovered a pattern conveying the restriction of their mother's voice to private homebound matters, whereas their father's voice was that of authority both in the home and in the public world. As our discussions turned to the public world, they looked at me with a frightened realization that to be silenced meant exactly that: to have no voice, no choice around so many significant matters. The "daddy's-little-girl" role they had played for so long continued into the "real" world. Someone else knew better, was there to take care of them, and would surprise them with gifts (that is, of course, if they were good girls). These young women for the first time in their lives began to critically understand the social construction of their silencing. They looked at me in disbelief and asked, "How can this be, aren't women mostly equal today?"

I read to them Marge Piercy's poem, "Right to Life" taken from *The Moon Is Always Female* (1989, pp. 95-97). (With apologizes to Marge Piercy for this partial quote.)

> We are all born of woman, in the rose of the womb we suckled our mother's blood and every baby born has a right to love like a seedling to sun.
>
> Every baby born unloved, unwanted is a bill that will come due in twenty years with interest, an anger that must find a target, a pain that will beget pain. A decade downstream a child screams, a woman falls, a synagogue is torched, a firing squad is summoned, a button is pushed and the world burns.
>
> I will choose what enters me, what becomes flesh of my flesh. Without choice, no politics, no ethics live. I am not your cornfield, not your uranium mine, not your calf for fattening, not your cow for milking.
>
> You may not use me as your factory. Priests and legislators do not hold shares in my womb or my mind. This is my body. If I give it to you I want it back. My life is not a non-negotiable demand.

As the political implications of silence became clearer, I read another poem of Marge Piercy's, "For Strong Women."

> A strong woman is strong in words, in action, in connection, in feeling;... Until we are all strong together, a strong woman is a woman strongly afraid. (pp. 56-57)

They began to hear each other's oppression, recognizing it as their own. But mostly they began to feel the strength of relationships; the ties of solidarity woven through words of embarrassment, compassion, and fear. One dancer shares how she experiences speaking: "I feel like an inch tall and people will laugh at me and they will think I am stupid."

> Rising from their solitary positions on stage, two dancers begin patting their right feet, hands on hips, like impatient mothers. Others fling their right arms, taking them into defiant circles. The stage

comes alive. Dancers cross each other, sometimes moving together and sometimes changing movements, mimicking other dancers. They jump, throw their torsos forward and back, pulsating with the growing resistance they have come to know. Covering their mouths with their hands, they jerk their heads to the side and spin around moving to new spaces. Each one comes to stillness. Together they fall backwards catching themselves with their feet, leap into the air and come to the floor rolling right then left, standing to press the invisible wall with their hands.

I had given them two articles to read. One was Susan Brownmiller's chapter on "Voice" in her book *Femininity* (1984), and another from *Women's Ways of Knowing* (Belenky, Clinchy, Goldberger, & Tarule, 1986) called "Silence" that began with the quote from Adrienne Rich: *"Where language and naming are power, silence is oppression, is violence."* This sentence became symbolic of where we had come in our discussion. From these readings I ask the dancers to reflect upon these phrases: "Obeying Authority," "Words as Weapons," and "Seen but not Heard." My attempt was to bring to words their everyday experiences, recognizing that being silenced often requires collaboration and complicity that the cultural norms have structured and accepted as normalcy. The tendency of the dancers was to explain away the injustices in terms that naturalize them; "that's just how it is." I could hear them through their explanations struggling to hold on to the familiar. They instinctively knew that for them to recognize their subjugation demanded making a choice. Indecision meant complicity and conformity. Their stories continued: "You wouldn't believe what happened in class. This male professor told us we were just like sixth-grade girls," and "I spoke with my father and I made him hear what I was saying. For the first time he understood I meant what I said about teaching and how important it is to me." And questions came: "Why aren't there more women in Congress?"; "Why is the president of a woman's college a man?"; "Why don't men listen to women when they speak?" We talked about how the verbal capacity of women had been hindered in various areas—medicine, law, politics, art, and business.

As their questioning grew, so did their anger and frustration. And their dance movements took a resistant form:

> The stage is dark. Silhouettes are engraved on a golden background. Bodies are scattered in the darkness, signifying the unidentifiable persons; stripped of subjectivity. The crouched forms stamp, and extend arms and legs to check their boundaries. Quietly the sounds change from inchoate body-made noises into distinguishable words.
> "I didn't want to say anything because I didn't want to hurt his feelings."
> "She used silence as a way to communicate."
> "I just sat there."
> "He wouldn't listen to what I had to say. So I wouldn't say anything."
> "Among women you can still be silenced."

These sentences, developed from a reflective writing exercise, had been prerecorded and inserted into the dance performance. The dancers wrote about experiences in which they felt too embarrassed, shy, nervous, intimidated, or inadequate to speak or answer back. They were drawn from the context of school, work, family, friends, male relationships, and gynecological examinations. Reversing the process of drawing words from their reflections to create movement, I asked them to move their memories of their embodied feelings. After they had created their movements they were to reflect upon them and make sense of what they had learned from their bodies about their lives through this process. The power of drawing upon body-knowledge gave the dancers a new understanding of what this might mean. Rather than their bodies being objects for technical proficiency (the dominant concern in dance), they became the vehicle for critical understanding of their life-world. They came to understand, through this process of recalling concrete body memories, how their own bodies held and mediated personal knowledge. They learned the meaning of the body as the materiality of existence. *They came to know themselves as body/subjects*:

> Slowly the silhouettes are lit, revealing parts of bodies. The dancers call to each other in soft voices—crawling, reaching towards each other and forming a semicircle. The backdrop takes on a glow of fire. They sit, legs open out to the side, feet touching feet. They acknowl-

edge each other. Fingernails consecutively tap the floor—again displaying impatience. Hands slapping interrupts as a pounding rhythm is established. Louder and louder, sounding their determination. Two dancers fall over to the floor on their sides, legs flinging, leading their bodies into rolls, right then left. Others join. It is a primal gathering evoking a time prior to mind/body dualisms. Each dancer takes her turn marking the circle. Crouched, their hands touch the floor quickly one after the other moving the circular pattern. A unity is formed. They come to stillness, backs to the audience, sitting cross-legged. Together their arms take on a methodical pattern—one that traces an arch of the energy that surrounds them. Their arms gathers up the energy into their center of being, and release it in an upward motion. It travels through their bodies and out their fingertips. The movement images a calling together of community and power. One after the other they come to standing, criss-crossing the stage, running, though not away. They end one behind the other in a line facing front. For the first time each dancer takes her turn directly facing the audience. In silence they make their presence known.

During our work together, I showed the film *Act of Passion*. Based upon a true story written by Heinrich Boll, it describes events that took place in West Germany in the mid 1960s. Kathyrn Beck is viciously and unjustly hounded by the police and media for her involvement with the political dissident Ben Cole. The film turns on her inability to persuade those men in authority or influence to listen to her story. The dancers reacted strongly to the injustices depicted in the film. As I listened I learned of their naive acceptance of bourgeois society's myths concerning issues of justice and tolerance. They were stunned by the utter powerlessness of even a middle-class white woman in the face of a predatory press and a sexist and repressive state. Their own experiences were stirred by the feelings of helplessness and total vulnerability as they recognized the ways in which women can be silenced.

Together in strength their bodies mark images of anger and resistance—a refusal of the dehumanizing act of silencing. Feet flex and push through the imaginary walls. They turn slipping through the cracks, releasing their bodies to move with the fullness of their own life energies. Defiantly they leap crossing the stage, landing, standing in solid form, gathering in solidarity as they face the audience front on—the silence. Hands covering their mouths, their eyes demand an answer—"Why?"

As I watched the performance I saw for the first time these young women publicly confessing their fears, pain, and anger. I came to know more about myself, others, and our shared culture. I sensed the similarities and differences. They have brought to form their inner lives which guide their actions in the social world. They have made connections, and cannot return to their former state of unawareness. There is, in addition, a process of bonding that takes place through this. We have come to trust and support each other, creating a safe place in which to strip away our protective layers. It is a place within where we may find new understandings as we hear our own voices recall and speak the knowledge of our bodies.

An interview is the final stage of the process. I developed a set of questions to encourage dialogue focused upon the issue of silencing, the pedagogic/choreographic process, and about feminism in general. My intention was to learn if, indeed, through this process, critical awareness of the issue has occurred; whether there was critical understanding of the relationship between the individual and culture, influencing what the students think, feel, and act upon; and, more importantly, if they have begun to find and hear their own voices and, as body/subjects, could become more empowered human beings.

This development of a critical pedagogy of the body differs from other choreographic processes in their use of personal memory to create movement. My intention here is directed toward self and social understanding for the purpose of social critique and political change. In the course of the pedagogic process, students came to see themselves in ways that were personally empowering and liberating. They were able to challenge some of the stereotypical notions of women's identities as sexual beings and gender roles. The process has also sought to develop a curriculum in dance that attends to the body as subject rather than as object; that is, one where the body is no longer simply a vehicle for performance, but rather a being engaged in the attempt to make meaning in the context of one's world. The dancer becomes an individual actively reflecting upon her social context; exploring what it means to be human in a world that limits women's freedom, value, and possibilities. The dancer, as anyone, is a self who lives experiences (Stinson, 1995). Finally, the process is one that nurtures a sense of connectedness and compassion among the dancers. It helps create what Sharon Welch has called "a community of resistance and solidarity." This dance, "Silent Voices," like my other work, challenges some of the traditional aesthetics of dance. It draws upon a Marxist aesthetics that is concerned with the dialectic between personal experience and the social world, inner sensibilities and outer context, and compels us to "make the familiar strange." Art, here, becomes integrally concerned with the process of healing and transforming our world.

Sentient Knowledge: Reclaiming a Discourse

It is important to reiterate here that notwithstanding what has been described above, most of what is found within dance education resembles Paulo Freire's notion of the "banking concept" of teaching. Students learn to silence their own voices, obey authority without questioning, fragment their being with the consequent separations of mind and body, rational and sensual, individual and social. We ask students to become bodiless beings or "no-bodies." We ask them to alienate themselves from their feelings—their aesthetic or bodily experiences from the emphasis on cerebral knowledge. As Stanley Keleman (1981) writes, "It's our emphasis on knowing that enables the brain to feel that it 'has' a body.... Then, rather than being some-body, we have a body" (p. 124). I am the body I live. There can be no separation. Technical form and pre-forming cannot replace our human capacity to create who we are and the world in which we live. And, art must be given broader significance—to help us understand something about the "what is" of our concrete lives, and to imagine and/or experience kinesthetically the possibilities for "what could or should be."

Quite obviously, however, the issues raised in this book take us beyond areas of the curriculum that are most clearly body-related. They compel us to question the historic denial of the body in our epistemological and educational concerns. Jane Roland Martin's (1993) concerns about the distinctions between what she calls "productive" and "reproductive" knowledge are important here. The former refers to the public world of work and politics, the latter to the private one of feeling, emotion, intimacy, and connection. In our culture's hierarchy of values, the productive processes of society and their associated traits are placed far ahead of the reproductive processes. To subordinate the latter, as we do, is to give little valence to the experience and knowledge of the body. And, says Martin, this is reflected in our education, which sees itself, preeminently, as the realm of the rational: "Feeling and emotion have no place in it, and neither do intimacy and connection. Instead analysis, critical thinking, and self-sufficiency are the dominant values" (p. 141). Alienation from the body will recur so long as we equate being an educated person with having a liberal education. Isolation and divorce from emotions will be repeated, says Martin, so long as we define education exclusively in relation to the productive processes of society:

> Education need not separate mind from body and thought from action, for it need not draw a sharp line between liberal and vocational education. More to the point, it need not separate reason from emotion and self from other. The reproductive processes *can* be brought into the educational realm thereby overriding the theoretical and practical grounds for ignoring feeling and emotion, intimacy and connection. (pp. 141-142)

We cannot underestimate the difficulties of such a change given the challenge this presents to the gender-related structure of material and ideological interests. Yet we must also be cognizant that the postmodern turn towards the body is more than a novel feature of the present cultural juncture. It is more like a return of the repressed in modernity—though this time with a decidedly anti essentialist flavor about what the body is or is not. It is a tendency that seems to express what Zygmunt Bauman (1991) has described as our ambivalence towards modernity's emphasis on cold hard rationality, order, and certainty. And, of course, in education the challenge of the body is not unrelated to that historically-rooted counter discourse that has always resisted those dualisms of mind and body, experience and knowledge, education and training, seeing in them the disfigurements of the human world. There is another narrative here of those teachers who have continually struggled to resist such distortions, impelled by a vision of human and social integrity, wholeness, and sensual being. The curriculum work described in this chapter, and the larger project of a critical pedagogy of the body from which it is derived, seeks to renew and enlarge just such a vision.

Conclusion: Remembering the Emancipatory Self

In the pursuit of such a vision the postmodern contribution is a limited one. While it has renewed and developed our interest in the body, it has, at the same time, continued the process of objectifying the body. This has been well described by Terry Eagleton (1996). He notes that the shift from Merleau-Ponty to Michel Foucault is one from the body as subject to the body as object:

> For Merleau-Ponty...the body is 'where there is something to be done'; for the new somatics, the body is where something—gazing, imprinting, regulating—is being done to you. It used to be called alienation, but that implies the existence of an interiority to be alienated, a proposition about which some postmodernism is deeply skeptical. (p. 71)

Eagleton notes that this view of the body is a heavily objectifying one, positioned as the end result of prior and external social processes. It seems to exclude any notion of what I have called in this book the "body/subject," which is to say, the body as a place from which human actions and creativity emanate.

> What is special about the human body...is just its capacity to transform itself in the process of transforming the material bodies around it. It is in this sense that it is anterior to those bodies, a kind of 'surplus' over and above them rather than an object to be reckoned up alongside

> them. But if the body is a self-transformative practice, then it is not identical with itself in the manner of corpses or carpets. (p. 72)

Eagleton notes that the human body is no simple object because it is the center from which significant projects are organized. Unlike objects, it is a creative being with a capacity to transcend our own "natures" or the context in which the body finds itself. Our lives are continually at risk because we have the capacity to transgress or transcend the place we find ourselves in. Like language the body/subject can liberate us from the prison house of our senses.

It is precisely in this argument with the postmodern tendency towards the objectification of the body that we should note Peter McLaren's important intervention. McLaren (in Biesta, 1995), too, asserts that we need a language that grasps the body in its capacity as an actor in history. He notes that there exists always a "margin" between the subject positions provided by the discourse and the way in which the "body/flesh" is inserted into this discourse.

> This margin is the effect of the impossibility of the exhaustion of the body/flesh in its representations. This margin expresses itself as *resistance* of the body/flesh, resistance against the insertion into the discourse. McLaren stresses that this resistance does not happen outside the body but operates as a tension within the body. (Biesta, p. 227)

McLaren's concept of subjectivity is no simple repeat of the Kantian version, that is, the autonomous, coherent and rational ego. Instead it starts with "the heteronomy of subjectivity," that is, human beings living their lives in opposition of resistance towards domination and repression. McLaren asserts that while human beings obviously do not constitute themselves—they are socially constituted—does not rule out the fact that human beings can be self-conscious. Indeed "self-consciousness and repression both play important roles in the constitution of the subject; it is exactly "the capacity of individuals to at least partially recognize the constitution of the self" that makes liberation possible" (in Biesta, p. 227-228).

Like this writer, Peter McLaren, as an advocate for critical pedagogy, knows that human beings are creatures of struggle, resistance, and the will to change their lives often in the face of enormous obstacles. Indeed without this sense of agency and power there can be no talk of emancipation and possibility, only the endless repetition of domination and constraint. While the will to self and social empowerment may be a less than fully conscious one, it is, nonetheless, ever present in the narrative of human existence. And in this narrative, bodies themselves often play a clear role in the assertion of freedom and transformation. McLaren notes that "critical pedagogy must grapple with the ways in which youth resist the dominant culture *at the level of their bodies* because in so doing the utopian moments to which such resistance points can be transformed pedagogically into strategies of empowerment" (in Biesta, p. 227). Yet my own experience in the field has taught me that "resistance" is perhaps a too-limited notion of what impels the struggle for change. There is more at stake here than simply opposing limits. Human subjectivity depends in the final analysis on a sense of identity—an identity that is nothing if it is not grounded in memory. Indeed, without memory there is no human consciousness and no human subjectivity. But memory is more than a record of resistance and pain. It is also (as Marcuse noted) the record of joy and pleasure; the latter is surely the font of our utopian hopes and dreams. In my work I am constantly reminded of just how much the body/subject draws energy and courage from the experience of both suffering *and* pleasure. The body memories that have been central to my pedagogy are, at least in part, a record of the felt world of self and other in all of its sensuous and relational qualities. It is surely the latter that grounds that desire for a different kind of world—one of compassion, love and justice. Re-membering in this sense becomes the act of re-identifying the self in all of its creative, critical, and ethical dimensions; it becomes the process of finding a home in this torn and afflicted world. It is "tikkun olam"—the repair and healing of the world.

My own work here has sought to attend to the importance of the body as a crucial, if neglected, vehicle for a critical pedagogy that wishes to make possible the re-thinking, and re-connecting of our moral, cognitive, and aesthetic selves. The haunting images of the deadened, lifeless bodies of our students in our classrooms or planted in front of televisions confronts us as educators. The task is larger than a cognitive repositioning of the historical and cultural subject. No longer can we suggest that the ability to rationally apprehend a situation is enough. The lack of desire, of feeling, of hope, of erotic life energies, puts before us a different kind of question and the need for a different kind of focus for our pedagogy. And it is this concern that has been central to my critical theory (as well as my own work as a teacher-educator in dance). Knowledge—albeit radical knowledge—without sensibility and sensuality leaves the cold, unfeeling shell of breathing flesh devoid of the capacity for love, suffering, joy, and compassion. A pedagogy concerned with human liberation must insist upon a sensual language and practice for education, which may evoke among our students a passion for love and justice; in which words spoken in our classrooms dance with the feelings of those life narratives that viscerally evoke the meaning, possibilities, and struggles for a freer, more compassionate and fully human life.

References

Aronowitz, S., & Giroux, H. (1991). *Postmodern education.* Minneapolis: University of Minnesota Press.

Bartky, S. (1990). *Femininity and domination.* New York: Routledge.

Baudrillard, J. (1983). *Simulations.* New York: Semiotext.

Baudrillard, J. (1981). For a critique of the political. *Economy of the sign.* St. Louis: Telos Press.

Bauman, Z. (1991). *Modernity and ambivalence.* Ithaca: Cornell University Press.

Belenky, M., Clinchy, B., Goldberger, N., & Tarule, J. (1986). *Women's ways of knowing.* New York: Basic Books.

Berger, J. (1984). *And our faces, my heart, brief as photos.* New York: Pantheon.

Biesta, G. (1995). The identity of the body." In M. Katz (Ed.), *Philosophy of Education 1994*. (pp. 223-232). Illinois: Philosophy of Education Society.

Bordo, S. (1993). *Unbearable weight*. Los Angeles: University of California Press.

Bordo, S. (1990). Feminism, postmodernism, and gender-skepticism. In L. Nicholson (Ed.) *Feminism/Postmodernism*. New York: Routledge.

Brownmiller, S. (1984). *Femininity*. New York: Ballantine.

Burbules, N., & Rice, S. (1991). Dialogue across differences: Continuing the conversation. *Harvard Educational Review*, 61(4), 393-416.

Butler, J. (1993). *Bodies that matter: On the discursive limits of "sex."* New York and London: Routledge.

Eagleton, T. (1996). *The illusions of postmodernism*. Oxford, UK: Basil Blackwell.

Eagleton, T. (1991). *Ideology: An introduction*. London: Verso.

Eagleton, T. (1990). *The ideology of the aesthetic*. Cambridge: Basil Blackwell.

Eagleton, T. (1985). The subject of literature. *Cultural Critique*, 2, 95-104.

Ellsworth, E. (1989). Why doesn't this feel empowering? Working through the repressive myths of critical pedagogy. *Harvard Educational Review*, 59, 297-324.

Foucault, M. (1980). *Power/knowledge: Selected interviews and other writings 1972-1977*. New York: Pantheon.

Freire, P. (1988). *Pedagogy of the oppressed*. New York: Continuum.

Gatens, M. (1996). *Imaginary bodies: Ethics, power, and corporeality*. New York and London: Routledge

Gilligan, C. (1990). Joining the resistance; psychology, politics, girls and women. The female body, *Michigan Quarterly Review*, XXIX (4), 501-536.

Giroux, H.A., & McLaren, P. (1994). *Between borders*. New York: Routledge.

Giroux, H. (1992). *Border crossings: Cultural workers and the politics of education*. New York: Routledge.

Giroux, H. (Ed.). (1988). Schooling in the postmodern age. *Journal of Education*, 170(3).

Greene, M. (1988). *The dialectic of freedom*. New York: Teachers College Press.

Grosz, E. (1994). *Volatile bodies: Toward a corporeal feminism.* Bloomington and Indianapolis: Indiana University Press.

Harding, S. (1990). Feminism, science, and the antienlightenment critiques. In L. Nicholson (Ed), *Feminism/Postmodernism,* (pp. 83-106). New York: Routledge.

Harvey, D. (1989). *The condition of postmodernity*. Oxford: Basil Blackwell.

hooks, b. (1990). *Yearning*. Boston: South End Press.

Hutcheon, L. (1989). *The politics of the postmodern*. London: Routledge.

Kariel, H. (1989). *The desperate politics of postmodernism.* Amherst: University of Massachusetts.

Keleman, S. (1981). *Your body speaks its mind*. Berkeley: Center Press.

Kellner, D. (1988). Reading images critically: Towards a postmodern pedagogy. *Journal of Education*, 170(3), pp. 31-52.

Lowe, D.M. (1995). *The body in late-capitalist U.S.A.* Durham, NC: Duke University Press.

Luke, C., & Gore, J. (Eds.). (1992). *Feminism and critical pedagogy*. New York: Routledge.

Lyotard, J-F. (1984). *The postmodern condition*. Minneapolis: University of Minnesota Press.

Martin, J. (1993). Becoming educated: A journey of alienation or integration? In S. Shapiro and D. Purpel (Eds.), *Critical social issues in American education*. pp. 137-148. New York: Longman.

McLaren, P. (1988). Schooling the postmodern body: Critical pedagogy and the politics of enfleshment. *Journal of Education*, 170(3), 53-83.

Middleton, S. (1993). *Educating feminists*. New York: Teachers College Press.

Nicholson, L. (1990). *Feminism/Postmodernism*. New York: Routledge.

Piercy, M. (1989). *The moon is always female.* New York: Knopf.

Rifkin, J. (1991). *Biosphere politics.* New York: Crown.

Rosenau, P. (1992). *Postmodernism and the social sciences.* Princeton: Princeton University Press.

Shapiro, Sherry. (1996). Towards transformative teachers: Critical and feminist perspectives in dance education. *Impulse* (1) pp. 37-48.

Shapiro, Sherry. (1995). Studies in dancer's lives: Feminist and postmodern perspectives. *Research Quarterly for Exercise and Sport Abstracts Supplement.*

Shapiro, Sherry. (1995). Skinned alive: Towards a postmodern pedagogy of the body. In P. McLaren (Ed.), *Postmodernism, postcolonialism, and pedagogy* (pp. 101-120). Australia: James Nicholas Publishers.

Shapiro, Sherry, & Shapiro, H. Svi. (1995). Silent voices; bodies of knowledge: Towards a critical pedagogy of the body. *Journal of curriculum theorizing,* (1)pp. 49-72.

Shapiro, H. Svi. (1991). Postmodernism and the crisis of reason: Social change or the drama of the aesthetic? *Educational Foundations,* 5(4), 53-68.

Smart, B. (1992). *Modern conditions, postmodern controversies.* London: Routledge.

Stinson, S. (1995). Body of Knowledge, *Educational Theory,* 45(1), pp. 43-54.

Taylor (Shapiro), Sherry. (1994). Reaching beyond the familiar: Redefining dance education as an emancipatory pedagogy. *Comunicacoes & Artes,* (Translated into Portuguese by Isabel Marques), 17,(28) pp. 65-76.

Weiler, K. (1988). *Women Teaching for Change.* Massachusetts: Bergin & Garvey.

Welch, S. (1990). *A feminist ethic of risk.* Minneapolis: Fortress Press.

Welch, S. (1985). *Communities of solidarity and resistance.* New YorSk: Orbis.

Index

moral: concerns, 15; judgement,
    93; questions, 39-40
Morales, Richard, 123
Morrison, Toni, 79-80
movement, 156; and language,
    136-137

naming, 59-60, 121
narcissism, 127
natality, 122
nature, fear of, 93
Nazis, 39
nonauthentic modes of being, 85
North Carolina, 6

objectification of body, 45, 60-63,
    127; history of, 45-47; resis-
    tance to, 116-123
objectified images, 64
oneness, 99
ontology, 3-4
oppression, 9, 24, 50, 54-55;
    class, 65; and economic sys-
    tem, 55-56; and participation,
    60-63
"Our Grandmothers", 67-69

Pacino, Al, 127
paradigm shift, 4
participation: in choreographic
    process, 150; in oppression,
    60-63
patriarchy, 9, 47-48, 53
pedagogy of enfleshment, 145
physical culture, 105
Piercy, Marge, 154-155
Pinar, William, 59
place, 115-117
play, 85-86, 96
poetics of revolution, 98

political change, 158
politics, 35-36
popular culture, 12-13, 71-72
possibility, 7-8, 17, 122-123; and
    critique, 9; and power, 71; and
    reason, 35-35
post-instrumentality, 96
postmodern: critique, 146; decon-
    struction, 35-36; discourse,
    19-20; life-world, 34-35; the-
    orists, 77-80; thinking, 4, 64,
    142, 144; turn toward body,
    160-161
postmodernism, 53-54
power, 7, 15, 54, 58, 147-149;
    and body, 50; and feeling, 98;
    and feminist critique, 35-36;
    and language, 25; male, 60-
    61; and patriarchal discourse,
    32; and possibility, 7; and
    relations, 50; and resistance,
    111
power/knowledge, 142-144
praxis, 10, 17-18, 81, 143
private/public, 45-51
problematizing, 11, 12
productive knowledge, 160
Purpel, David, 14, 18

questioning, 4, 136, 153-154,
    155-156

race, 54-60, 67-69
radical democracy, 9
reality, 3-4, 22, 26, 34, 65-66,
    115-116, 143-144
reason, 78; cynical, 69-74; and
    logos, 39-41; and possibility,
    35-35; sensual, 35; and sup-
    pression of desire, 45-51